BARE-KNUCKLE
NEGOTIATION

BARE – KNUCKLE NEGOTIATION

Savvy Tips and True Stories from
the Master of Give-and-Take

Raoul Felder

WILEY

JOHN WILEY & SONS, INC.

Published by John Wiley & Sons, Inc., Hoboken, New Jersey.
Published simultaneously in Canada.

For general information on our other products and services please contact our Customer Care Department within the United States at (800) 762-2974, outside the United States at (317) 572-3993 or fax (317) 572-4002.

Wiley also publishes its books in a variety of electronic formats. Some content that appears in print may not be available in electronic books. For more information about Wiley products, visit our web site at www.wiley.com.

Library of Congress Cataloging-in-Publication Data:

Felder, Raoul Lionel, 1934–
    Bare-knuckle negotiation : savvy tips and true stories from the master
of give-and-take / Raoul Felder.
        p.   cm.
    Includes index.
    ISBN 0-471-46333-7 (CLOTH)
    1. Felder, Raoul Lionel, 1934–   2. Public prosecutors—New York
(State)—New York—Biography.   3. Lawyers—New York (State)—New
York—Biography.   4. Compromise (Law)   5. Negotiation.   I. Title.
KF373.F38A33 2004
347.73′9′092—dc22

                                                                    2003018879

Printed in the United States of America.

10 9 8 7 6 5 4 3 2 1

For the next generation of negotiators,
especially my granddaughter Millie,
who is the best negotiator of all—even before she
was able to talk, she was able to get whatever
she wanted. But I am a sucker for a pretty face.

CONTENTS

FOREWORD

There is a lot I can say on the subject of negotiation, but at these prices, why should I?

Artists and performers, as a class, have been exploited because of their lack of self-confidence and limited negotiating ability. For the most part, they lack the necessary skills to arrive at some fair recognition for their artistry. Early in my own career, I traveled the small towns of the South and up and down the eastern seaboard. I can't recall the number of times I have been called a "bastard."

Years ago, many young performers (and especially, African Americans) basically were at the mercy of the gentlemen controlling the record companies and nightclubs (translation: the dese and dose guys of the bent-nose crowd who offered propositions you couldn't refuse). Even later in their careers, successful artists were subject to exploitation and misuse.

For example, let's say a big star got $300,000 per performance. The star's manager negotiated to have a lavender piano in the dressing room, polka-dotted walls, and hot and cold running members of the opposite sex. Ten minutes of thought would make it obvious that the person paying (who also ran the show) was going to include the cost of these extras in the bottom number on the total budget. So the performer who made these sorts of demands received less and did not realize it, and the manager took bows for the lavender piano.

Personally, right now, I'm so big that wherever I go I ask Felder to accompany me to negotiate any problems along the way. But then again, I also have bodyguards, and the truth is, with bodyguards you don't have many problems left to negotiate. But then you would not need a big-name negotiator. Seriously, I have read this book and it is an invaluable guide to those situations where people can control their own destiny, and it is a tribute to what you can do if you master the art of negotiations. Now, Raoul, can I have my money?

JACKIE MASON

ACKNOWLEDGMENTS

I am especially grateful to Matthew Holt, Senior Editor of the Professional/Trade Group at John Wiley & Sons, Inc. He shepherded this project from beginning to end and offered many positive and constructive comments. His enthusiasm was always a source of encouragement.

Four good friends—great negotiators all—contributed passages in this book. I am indebted to Howard Koeppel, Randy Levine, Michael Hess, and Jeffery Shapiro for their contributions.

Allyn Freeman was helpful with research and organization, and Tamara Hummel at Wiley also deserves my gratitude.

INTRODUCTION

I was born to negotiate. It is in the Felder blood.

Some people presume that I acquired the tough negotiation street smarts of the inner city, growing up in the Williamsburg section of Brooklyn during the Great Depression. Popular inventive fiction likes to attach this quaint fable to people born and raised in the stickball-playing boroughs of New York.

The truth is more prosaic: I learned the skills of a good negotiator from my father, Morris, who was also an attorney. From the time I was six or seven years old, I used to listen on the other side of the door as my father talked to clients in our living room. What impressed me most was that people would arrive at our home displaying anger or anxiety, but after they talked with my father, most of their negative feelings would vanish. He could negotiate away their animosity and find the right path for an equitable settlement.

My father's law office was in our home, a common arrangement in the early 1940s. Like many other lawyers struggling to earn a living, he could not afford to rent outside space. I find it ironic that today rich and famous lawyers see clients at home; presumably some cachet exists by conducting business in the kitchen pantry, the library, or on the veranda.

MY BROTHER, THE NEGOTIATOR

I also learned the strength and power of negotiations from my late brother, Jerome. He was better known to the world as *Doc Pomus*, the songwriter of such famous hit tunes as "Save the Last Dance for Me," "A Teenager in Love," "This Magic Moment," and "Viva Las Vegas." He invented the professional handle of "Doc" to prevent neighbors and relatives from discovering that Mr. and Mrs. Felder's nice boy Jerome sang the blues in black nightclubs, where he was known as a "blues shouter."

Jerome had contracted polio in childhood and walked with cumbersome metal braces and crutches. Each day, he struggled to live as normal a life as possible. He used negotiation to acquire power over his handicap since every aspect of his existence required some form of give-and-take. Fifty years ago, there were no wheelchair ramps on city streets, no electrically powered wheelchairs, no lifts to access public buses, and no specialized van services for the handicapped. Life was a constant hell, and he had to depend on charm and verbal skills to accomplish the most basic tasks.

Finding a taxi was a daily challenge for Jerome. The cabs in our Brooklyn neighborhood cruised the pedestrian traffic beneath the Broadway elevated ("El") tracks several blocks away from our house. I learned how to hail a taxi on Broadway and would bribe the cabdriver with extra cash to come to our house and pick up my brother. Cabbies did not want to stop for handicapped people because it took extra time and they lost revenue picking up and dropping off a slow-moving person.

Home delivery services for food, drugs, books, and dry cleaning also were hard to come by in my brother's time; arranging for a delivery usually required the promise of a substantial bonus payment.

A mom-and-pop candy store was located about a block away from our house. My brother often did not have enough money to buy a full pack of cigarettes and, instead, bought a few at a time (called "looseys") for a penny apiece. Or he would telephone Mrs. Zimmerman, the storeowner, and plead for her to deliver five cigarettes to our house. But she always protested until he began negotiations, which usually involved an offer to give her a record as well as the promise to pay double for a pack of cigarettes the next time he visited her store.

Jerome's condition required him to live in elevator buildings all his life. When he had become a successful songwriter, his inability to climb stairs ended an infuriating and frivolous lawsuit. A mercenary saphead sued my brother and his publishing company claiming that Jerome had stolen the song "Save the Last Dance for Me" from the man's father. This jerk had never met Jerome and was unaware of his physical limitations. At the deposition, the man testified that Jerome came to his father's apartment where his dad played the song, and afterward my brother stole it. Jerome's attorney asked the man to describe the apartment, and he answered that it was on the third floor of a brownstone. The lawyer attached a doctor's medical certificate to the motion for dismissal on the commonsense grounds that a person with braces and metal crutches as a result of polio could not have walked up those three flights of stairs. Case dismissed.

In recording contracts at that time, an artist had to commit to a certain number of personal appearances in public to sing and promote a record. My brother always agreed to a more generous schedule of these performances than other artists. For this additional commitment, the recording studios paid him a bonus, delighted by his willingness to do more promotions. Once they discovered that he walked on crutches, however, they realized the difficulty and inadvisability of sending him on promotional tours so he kept the extra cash without having to travel.

A record company withdrew one of my brother's minor hits even though it was moving up the charts. The not-so-brilliant reasoning of these record executive "nappy rabbits" was that teenagers would not want to buy a record made by a handicapped person. Somebody should tell this news to Ray Charles and Stevie Wonder.

A Shortcut

I shall not characterize my life's experience as an upward journey from moderate circumstances in Brooklyn to a position of peer and public recognition. Only the fullness of time can permit such judgment. But I can say that any rewards I have gained are the result of learning and using negotiation skills. And many of these I owe to my father and brother.

You, too, can become an excellent negotiator, capable of playing a winning hand in life.

I offer this book as a shortcut.

LIFE IS A MINEFIELD

I have wanted to write a book about negotiation for a long time because life is a minefield. A person who does not know how to negotiate the perilous landscape of life can end up unhappy emotionally, legally, or economically, and can suffer personal damage to pride and self-esteem.

Several books have been published about the art of negotiation. To be blunt, these tomes are garbage, often written by university professors who have learned what little they know—or think they know—from other books written by similar academicians. None of these people have labored with insight or acumen in the field.

True to the way the United States conducts business, corporations that look for a negotiator often turn to academia. They rely on the false premise that somebody who is a professor in a particular subject must be proficient. The expert takes the assignment and then uses the work as confirmation of ability to perform such tasks. The process represents a perfect circle of the blind teaching the blind, who are then hired by the gullible.

Throw those books away!

I have negotiated billions of dollars, most often paid by a person who would have preferred to pay nothing. I have negotiated settlements for homes and boats, interests in businesses, patents, pets (including a parrot, Scottish terrier, and a boa constrictor), furniture, jewelry, and a piece of the Berlin Wall; child custody and visitation rights; monies that allegedly did not exist; free airline miles; vehicles (from a Rolls-Royce and electric scooters to a private railroad car and a Boeing 727 airplane); the value of legal, medical, and veterinary practices; who will do the dishes; where people will live or work; who will pay for hair plugs; the dollar value of celebrity in every profession from authors to movie stars; membership in country clubs, rubber rooms, and S&M dungeons; and collections of items ranging from toy trains, antique weather vanes, and biscuit tins to antique armor.

I am familiar with razor-sharp applications of negotiation skills for all occasions, legal and otherwise. Over the years, I have learned many proved and successful negotiation practices and have invented several new ones. Some of the concepts involve straightforward common sense and a few are devious and cunning. But they all work; take my word for it.

When people brag about their ability to negotiate, they often sound like people who boast about how they perform sex. They proudly proclaim how well they do it—but just completing the act does not mean it was a bravura performance.

Negotiation is both an art and a skill. A truism is that some people have the ability to negotiate and others do not. In more than 40 years of practicing law, I have witnessed some of the great negotiators in action and have seen firsthand the favorable results of their expertise.

Gaining Power

I graduated from the New York University Law School in 1959 and practiced law with my father from 1959 to January 1961. Then I joined the Department of Justice headed by Attorney

General Robert Kennedy. I became a prosecutor in the U.S. Attorney's office and was a member of the nation's first Organized Crime Task Force. I was also in charge of Federal Juvenile Delinquency, prosecuting for a geographic area that included millions of people.

During my introduction to the practice of criminal law, I became aware that defense lawyers had no power; the legal deck, so to speak, was stacked in favor of the government. Prosecutors tended to move forward those cases they were confident of winning; it was the "shooting the fish in the barrel" syndrome. When I practiced in the U.S. Attorney's office, most of the prosecutors wanted to try drug cases because if they could present drug evidence to the jury, it was sufficient to convict the defendant.

Once while summing up to a jury, I held up a large glassine bag containing a substantial amount of heroin. I had thought that it would be dramatic to have it passed around the jury (which did not happen). During summation, therefore, I dangled the bag about a foot over the table in front of the jury box. Then, in an attempt to be even more shocking, I dropped it on the table. I wanted the jurors to hear and remember a resounding *thud* that would reinforce the large quantity of heroin inside. When the bag hit the table, however, it burst open splattering the white powder over the jury and me. One might believe that this was one of the happiest juries ever impaneled.

In the 1960s, U.S. prosecutors with weak or unwinnable cases developed methods to decline prosecution. To make this happen, the prosecutor had to go through the pecking order at the federal headquarters of the Department of Justice. The paradox was that some of the lawyers who sat in positions of authority at the department—those who could yea and nay the prosecution of a case—had little or no prosecutorial experience. Often these attorneys worked at Justice because of political clout. Therefore, if a lawyer could forward enough convoluted reasons for not prosecuting the case, the request to drop it usually would receive approval.

Another delaying method at Justice was to change the tasks for each case every month. To holdup action, lawyers would write, "awaiting Grand Jury action," "interviewing witnesses," or "researching the law." Attorneys could prevent cases moving forward until they left the Department.

DEFENSE LAWYERS

Through my prosecutorial work, I came to appreciate the conduct and tactics of defense lawyers, which opened my eyes to the power of negotiation. These attorneys had to possess superior negotiation skills because often a plea bargain presented the only realistic chance to reduce their clients' sentences. Today, the obligatory minimum sentencing laws mandated by state and federal statutes have made plea skills even more necessary. The process has become a Hobson's choice for defense lawyers: Take a plea bargain or roll the dice for acquittal. But if they lose the case, the client can go to prison for many years.

The so-called Court Street defense lawyers in New York City handle nickel-and-dime blue-collar crime and low-end narcotics. These street-smart legal practitioners have been toughened in the legal trenches, and they know how to speak on behalf of their clients. They receive the same fee (essentially, all a poor client can afford) whether they negotiate a plea bargain or the case moves to trial.

OTHER TYPES OF LAWYERS

Some corporate lawyers possess poor negotiation skills. They work for the rich and powerful and occasionally forget whose money is at stake. These attorneys seem reluctant to put on the gloves and mix it up with a legal adversary because tough bargaining is beneath them. Their attitude is that give-and-take negotiations of the hard kind should occur in a criminal law practice and not a prestigious Wall Street or Park Avenue firm.

I also have observed that new lawyers are often knowledgeable about the law but do not understand the how and why of negotiations. These neophytes are equipped with erudite skills to argue law in front of the Supreme Court, but regrettably, they cannot find their way to the courthouse. They soon learn that most cases are settled through discussion and most disputes do not go to trial. I find it incongruous that law schools do not offer specific courses in negotiation although the greater part of American law seeks the private resolution of disagreements to prevent the parties ending up in a verdict after trial.

DIVORCE—OLDEN TIMES

When I began practicing, divorce law was to law as proctology was to medicine. Before the enactment of no-fault statutes, divorce lawyers developed an unsavory reputation. On the professional ladder, the public placed these practitioners somewhat lower than shady used car salesmen and higher than axe murderers. Adultery was the sole grounds for divorce in most states. The attorneys would arrange for a "raid" to take place at a motel or hotel. The prearranged and prepaid package included a cameraman, the private detective, the prostitute found in bed with the husband, and the photograph to be developed as proof and then destroyed. The process was so patently collusive that often there was a "key man" who could open the lock on the door (the husband had supplied the key beforehand) behind which the detective would "discover" the husband and the "girlfriend."

All to the better, this dirty era of the law has passed into history. On balance, new divorce laws are a substantial improvement on the old ones.

MODERN-DAY DIVORCE

The adoption of community property and equitable distribution statutes changed the status of divorce and also the standing of divorce lawyers. Divorce became profitable and respectable. Chief evidence of this new respectability is that corporate lawyers, who never would have touched the salaciousness of divorce before no-fault, now retain cases, or at least keep them for a longer period before referring them to a divorce lawyer. These firms use euphemisms like "family practice," "private law," and "private clients" to describe what everyone else labels plainly as divorce law or matrimonial law.

Ask divorce lawyers to estimate roughly the division of their practice between women and men, and the answer would be 80 percent—women, 20 percent—men. The reason for this wide discrepancy is that husbands often use the familiar services of their corporate or business attorneys, an opportunity that is unavailable to most nonworking wives. Wives seeking lawyers that specialize in divorce generate a list from people they know, from divorced female friends, or from articles about divorce cases in the popular press. Search methods today include surfing the Internet and watching legal shows on television that feature divorce.

DIVORCE LAW AS A TRAINING GROUND

My legal specialty is divorce, often referred to as a blood sport played out by hostile attorneys. The practice requires the combative skills of a pit bull and the Wisdom of Solomon; a smattering of the law also helps. No other legal field has as many areas of potential antagonism where conflicts can flare—husband versus wife, attorney versus attorney, attorney versus judge and, too often, clients versus their own lawyer.

In divorce law, we usually encounter two unhappy and hostile people, with husband and wife refusing to admit failure. The participants are bitter that what started out with love and closeness has degenerated into hate and separation. Emotions are raw, and at the outset, neither side wants to be conciliatory. Negotiation speeds the process to resolution, but not without pitfalls.

OBJECTS

When most other issues have been resolved, personal objects remain a contentious area because of the couple's emotional involvement with these items. This irrational attachment to things is idiosyncratic to divorce law. It does not matter whether the article is a valuable antique or a ten-cent knickknack, feuding parties in divorce will fight furiously for possession, often preferring to destroy the object than give it to the other party.

A divorce case of a well-known female advertising executive illustrates how high emotions can escalate when enmity and possession of objects clash. I represented her husband, called a "boy toy" by the media. The wife, whose age was somewhere between sixty and death, had met her future husband when he was nineteen and working in the mailroom of her agency. After the property settlement, one matter remained unresolved: Who would take possession of their Scottish terrier, a valuable dog descended from President Franklin Roosevelt's, Fala? The judge awarded the husband sole custody of the dog and ordered the wife to leave the animal at the man's new place of business. I overheard her whisper to her lawyer, "The judge did not say the dog had to be alive when I dropped it off." Her words shocked me since the couple had expressed affection for the pet. I repeated this cruel statement to the judge, who issued a stern warning to the wife.

In New York State, a famous divorce case reached the highest appellate court because the divorcing pair could not negotiate ownership of an obscure object called a *tantalus*—a locked case or sideboard for storing bottles of wine or liquor. How important could this wine cabinet have been in a person's life that the dispute reached the highest court in the state? I also know of cases where the lawyers (bear in mind that a lawyer, like crime, does not pay) have chipped in to pay for a contested object that stood as a hurdle (often, the last one) to resolution.

Smart judges leave personal property decisions until the end of the divorce proceedings. They know from experience that important domestic issues (e.g., child payments and disposition of marital assets) will proceed by negotiation toward a settlement because, at core center, money solves these problems. A New York judge said, "If it's trouble, throw money at it and the problem will go away."

The gnarly hitches occur over the division of personal property. To shortcut the process, judges often ask a husband and wife to submit a list of all the personal items acquired in a marriage that are in dispute and, in one or two sentences, indicate why a particular object is important and why he or she should receive it. I was in a judge's office on another case when he reviewed two long and detailed property lists from husband and wife. Without glancing at the emotional reasons each side had written for being awarded Uncle Berky's Tiffany lamp or Grandma Patch's Hoosier cabinet, the judge checked off the items one after the other. He awarded an object for the wife and then the next for the husband until he had completed the bottom page of the long lists. He said, "How sad they fight over the inconsequential debris of an ended marriage."

The point is never to want anything too much—with the emphasis on "thing."

Avoid Third-Party Arbiters

Always try to negotiate a satisfactory conclusion without the assistance of a third party. By agreeing to let some other person arbitrate the dispute, you relinquish control over the procedure and lose power. When a third person charts the course of resolution, the outcome becomes unpredictable.

People fail to realize that when they opt for a third party, the unknown factor is how that individual will feel on decision day. A judge who has had a bad morning with a spouse, child, or law clerk may not be in a mood to settle a dispute reasonably and fairly. This holds true for other third-party mediators as well, whether it involves requesting input from another fair-minded person or acceding to a child's wish for a parent to decide the dispute. The third person's emotional state on decision day is a crapshoot.

In some instances, employment and union contracts bind both parties to compulsory arbitration. This is a prime example eliminating the legal right of access to the judicial system with its safeguards and built-in impartiality. The supposition is that the arbitration process will be neutral and the outcome will be fair. Often, inequity is an inherent aspect of this third-party system because you choose an arbitrator for a one-time arbitration. Arbitrators, however, may sit on a dozen or more cases involving the same firm (your opponent in the arbitration) during the course of the year. Their income, to one degree or another, depends on whether the company agrees to use their services as arbitrators in future matters.

Negotiations 101

My friend Randy Levine is the president of the New York Yankees and formerly served as New York's City Deputy Mayor for Economic Development, Planning and Administration. He has some helpful reminders about negotiation:

Negotiation is an art not a science. There is no strict formula to the process, just some basic and fundamental rules that you play by ear. Although you're an advocate for a certain position, you have to enter into negotiations with an open mind:

- Clear your mind. You can't be too fixed in your own judgment.
- Listening is much more important than talking. When you listen, you can hear not only the other persons' stated goal but also often what they're trying to achieve.
- Always maintain your credibility. Never agree to something that you can't or won't deliver.
- Be flexible. You can't get everything you want. Sometimes it's not good to achieve all your goals at the other person's expense.
- Never be afraid to adjust your goals. You can always say, "I was wrong about this point at the start of the negotiations." You have to realize the other person has a position, too.

DEALING WITH ODDBALLS

Although few laypeople today remember the late Harry Lipsig, who practiced negligence law in New York, in his prime he was a legend. One still hears his name when lawyers gather, "And tell sad stories of the death of kings."

Often referred to as "The King of Torts," *New York Magazine* described him as "the toughest, and most successful personal injury specialist in the country." He was 5 feet 1 inch tall and sat in his office like a Napoleon on a mammoth throne-like chair of tufted black leather. Despite his diminutive height, he was an imposing presence, a clotheshorse dandy who used his size as a power advantage.

During a lengthy and distinguished legal career, Lipsig won hundreds of millions—even billions—of dollars for his clients. But during the last years of his life, he relied on a bizarre behavioral pattern to negotiate with other attorneys: He conversed in doggerel. The patter might go something like this:

In my office I see Mr. Raoul Felder,
He thinks he's as smart as Pliny, the Elder.
But he's a lawyer, who gets in my craw,
Today I'll clean his clock with the law.

Discussions with Lipsig were a challenge because it was difficult to keep focused on the legal issues while he spoke in appalling rhymed couplets.

During one meeting in his predoggerel days, I was present
when a lawyer entered the office to announce that the firm's
client had turned down a resolution of a drawn-out case in which
both attorneys had agreed to a settlement. Lipsig was irate and
shouted, "Damn! Damn! Raoul, the source of our trouble in this
business is . . . [and he groped in air to pull the right word until it
came out] . . . is *clients!*"

On another occasion early in my career, my opponent in a divorce case was the great attorney Louis Nizer, a recognized legal
authority on contracts, copyright, plagiarism, and public relations.
His most celebrated case—a successful libel suit by Quentin
Reynolds against conservative journalist Westbrook Pegler—was
later memorialized in a Broadway play *A Case of Libel.* Nizer was
also an author of two best-selling books about the law *My Life in
Court* and *The Jury Returns.* In his day, he was the most recognized
and famous lawyer in the United States.

We had negotiated a settlement, and I went to his office in the
old Paramount Building on Times Square with the papers for signing. Minutes passed, and my client failed to arrive. Fifteen minutes
later, she called to cancel the meeting. In the taxi ride to Nizer's
office, she had read her horoscope in the *New York Daily Mirror,*
which counseled against making any life decisions on that day.

I related my client's horoscope quandary to Nizer with much
embarrassment. He shrugged his shoulders and said, "Some
clients are so peculiar, you have to know if they're allergic to your
aftershave lotion." (This may be one reason I grew a beard.)

I followed Nizer's advice and always delved into the professional backgrounds, health condition, and idiosyncrasies of my legal opponents, their clients, and even my own. Knowledge is power, and time and again, some insignificant tidbit of information provided me with a wedge to negotiate for victory.

RESEARCH

Another horoscope case shows the benefit of inquiry and research. I was involved in a child custody case in Upper Westchester, New York, where the wife of my client repeatedly postponed and rearranged court dates. The time I was wasting because of these chronic delays made me livid. When I asked what was causing the erratic scheduling, my client explained that an advisor astrologer's interpretation of the Zodiac influenced his wife's everyday existence. She never left home without a positive reading. Like most astrologers, this woman's stargazer based her recommendations on the position of planets at the particular time and place of the subject's birth. All astrologers rely on ancient texts, and this one used a book from the eighteenth century.

The next time we met in court, I consulted a retired professor of astronomy from Columbia University. I did not ask his personal opinion on the Zodiac; I knew he would say it was nonsense. Instead, I handed him copies of horoscopes of people born around the same time as my client's wife. These horoscopes all discussed certain planets in relation to other planets. I asked the professor if all of the planets mentioned in the horoscopes had been known at the time the book was published. The professor replied that when this "authoritative text" was written, three planets had not yet been discovered: Uranus in 1781, Neptune in 1846, and Pluto in 1930.

In court, I argued that the wife's reasons were bogus for postponing the court dates if she depended on advice from her astrologer, who, in turn, relied on a book about planets that was as believable as storks delivering babies. The professor's testimony accomplished more than I had anticipated because the court record now included statements showing the lack of common sense that governed the wife's life and her decisions. This information would affect her credibility as a fit parent in the custody case.

I had yet another odd custody case involving an astrologer. This mother also seemed to be under a stargazer's total control. After the husband gave us the wife's date of birth, we obtained her birth certificate from the Board of Health to determine the exact hour and minute because the time is always indicated on that document. I then hired a female private detective, who went to this particular astrologer for a reading and secretly taped the conversation.

At the meeting, as we anticipated, the astrologer asked for the day, date, and hour of the woman's birth. When my private detective revealed the exact birth time, day, and date of the wife, the astrologer was shocked, saying, "I have never seen a case like this. Believe it or not, I am now counseling your astrological twin." She admitted how much the other woman relied on the astrologer to handle life's most intimate details, including how to raise her child. Further, the astrologer boasted that she "controlled" the custody case by following the stars and the planets. We played the tape in court to my client's advantage. He won custody, and in truth, he was the more fit parent.

Arbitration 101

Years ago, I believed that my stockbroker cheated me by churning my portfolio, which cost me considerable money. The stockbroker, who worked for a large brokerage firm, was indicted by the U.S. government, tried, and was acquitted, although in my opinion she did not deserve that verdict.

After I complained to the company, this stockbroker refused to send me records of my prior trades. I taped her refusal when I recorded the telephone conversation. If the broker is a big income producer, the firm looks the other way, even if churning accounts was the modus operandi for a large number of trades.

I wanted to sue this firm but could not bring legal action because of the compulsory arbitration process. I ruminated that the panel of arbitrators available to me included the same people on hand for every other dissatisfied customer. We clients had one-shot deals with members on the panel, whereas the stockbroker's firm could choose from a small group of potential arbitrators who sat repeatedly on disputes involving the company. Which side had a better shot at a fair resolution with this panel of arbitrators?

Ask your stockbroker what happens if you disagree with investment advice offered by the firm. You will be informed that in the small print of the purchase agreement (in minuscule 2-point pica), you concurred to compulsory arbitration to settle disputes. It is a flagrant example of yielding control to a third party.

Scull Session

In 1985, we won the appeal of art patron Ethel Scull, who had previously lost her case when other attorneys represented her in court. We argued that she had not received a fair share of the artwork from her dissolved marriage to New York City taxi fleet tycoon, Robert Scull. In the 1960s, the couple was at the forefront of the Pop Art movement through their association with and patronage of Andy Warhol, Robert Rauschenberg, Jasper Johns, Roy Lichtenstein, and other emerging Pop artists. The Sculls were nouveau riche and enjoyed wide media attention.

Ethel had to file for an appeal because the initial proceedings denied her a fair percentage of the artworks she and her husband collected as partners during the marriage. We won in the intermediate appellate court, which reversed the trial court's decision.

Next, Robert Scull's lawyers appealed to the highest court in the state, the New York Court of Appeals. Robert Scull died two days before the final appeal was heard, but I believe he knew his ex-wife would win that appeal.

Once the case had been adjudicated in our favor, the judge ordered the equal division of artwork based on the appraised value. The sum was in the high millions of dollars as quoted in the official appraisal by Sotheby's, the renowned art appraisers and auction house.

We researched the entire collection and discovered, with Ethel's help, that a similar painting by Jasper Johns listed by Sotheby's earlier for a $1 million, had increased significantly to $1.8 million. In the intervening years after the first appraisal, demand for the painter's works had skyrocketed. Over time, his paintings sold at auction for high numbers, thus raising the value of his other works, including this painting. Everyone realized that whoever picked the first work of art from the estate (i.e., the Johns painting), would gain an instant bonus of at least $800,000.

Robert Scull's lawyers agreed to flip a coin to see who would choose the first painting. The coin tossing for millions would take place at an art warehouse in New York. The night before, I flipped a quarter for several hours, keeping track of the results. I concluded that if I started with the head side palm up, the outcome would be tails more than 50 percent of the time. I thought these skewed results probably occurred because the raised head side (George Washington's profile) contained a tad more metal, which would favor landing facedown.

On the day of the flip, I noticed that the quarter rested in the fingers of Robert Scull's lawyer with Washington's profile side up. I called tails. He flipped and dropped the coin, which rolled under a table. On the second toss, I again spotted the profile, called tails, and won. My first pick was the undervalued Jasper Johns, and Ethel had a serendipitous windfall of $800,000.

After the coin flip for the Johns work, we proceeded in lottery fashion to select the other paintings. All of the Sculls' art resided in a vast warehouse space alongside works from other collectors. As the lawyers made one selection after another, workers carried the pieces to other, smaller rooms, one rented by Robert Scull's estate and the other by Ethel Scull. Over time, the "his" and "hers" rooms filled, and the central space emptied of artwork.

On completion of the last transfer, the storage company turned out the lights in the large almost empty room, leaving a single bulb lit in the outside hallway. As I left the darkened room, I tripped over what appeared to be a large piece of oddly shaped lumber. At a glance, it resembled a piece of driftwood tangled in rope. I angrily kicked it off to the side, and when I reached the hallway, I told a warehouse executive that he should get rid of this leftover carpenter junk because someone could trip, fall, and sue. He entered the vast room to see what I was talking about and returned to inform me that the piece of junk I had tripped on and casually tossed aside was an expensive Rauschenberg construction. That's the trouble with being a Philistine.

By not being fair to his wife from the beginning of the divorce, Robert Scull had placed the ultimate decision in the hands of a third party and lost. Remember, results can go off into left field when someone else is the referee.

Everything Is Negotiable

When I tell people that I bargained for an expensive item at Tiffany's or Harry Winston's, they seem shocked and say, "Oh, Raoul, you can't do that." But, in truth, you can. You can negotiate for almost anything.

In our American culture, we don't bargain or hassle over a price at retail except in the new and used car market. We spot a price tag on an expensive item in a reputable shop, and our first thought is whether it is a fair value for the price. We do not realize that we can negotiate the price downward in a luxury store.

I am not implying that someone can haggle over the menu price of a pastrami sandwich at the Carnegie Deli. That is not feasible. But with some high-ticket items, bargaining is possible. The higher priced the item, the greater the likelihood of lowering the price. A smaller margin still can generate a handsome profit for the store. And here's a surprise; rich people may be different from you but not from me—they are not embarrassed to negotiate.

A proved technique at prestigious stores is to ask for the specific department's buyer. Salespeople do not have the authority to bargain so do not waste time with these clerks; deal only with decision makers. Start negotiation by pointing to the expensive item and say, "I would like to buy this piece but the price is too high. I know you are flexible so I am asking if you would take 'x' dollars less for a cash sale today?" The worst outcome is that the buyer says "no." You will be surprised how often the buyer agrees to the sale at the price you offered.

Fancy Stores

Do not be intimidated by a fancy store. Even the most reputable high-class stores sometimes become involved in dubious transactions. It was a celebrated tale in New York that a noted fur store did a substantial business with the mistresses of wealthy men. At the women's request, the men would shop for a fur coat at this store. The sole reason for specifying this particular store was that the women could return the fur and receive the discounted value of the coat back in cash. The store ended up reselling the never worn fur as new and, in addition, pocketed the profit from the original sale.

Another legal case involved a wealthy client who kept receiving a bill for $120,000 from a world-famous jewelry store months after his divorce. I contacted the store, made a visit to see the manager, and discovered this story: This man's wife had picked out a huge emerald, which cost $900,000. She asked her husband to buy the stone, but he insisted she return to the store and offer half the sum, the maximum the husband would pay. She went back to the store and agreed to pay the full $900,000 price by giving a 50 percent down payment and paying the $450,000 balance over time in secret monthly payments of $30,000.

The store took the down payment and gave her a sales slip to show her husband, indicating the full price was $450,000. She signed a private memorandum with the store, clearly stating that the full price was $900,000. The sales slip pleased the husband, who boasted he had negotiated this famous store down by 50 percent—proof to him that big-name stores had enormous profit margins. The honest wife lived up to her promise and began paying the balance at the agreed-on monthly rate. But when the couple divorced, she told the store to bill her husband for the balance.

I remember shopping for a painting at an art gallery where I overheard the owner talking to an heiress whom I had seen often at other galleries. As she quibbled about the price of a small Impressionist drawing, she asked for and received generous terms that allowed her to take possession of the work that day and pay monthly for the next two years. The owner acceded to every one of her negotiated demands.

Two for the Money

The Broadway producer Jyll Rosenfeld is a foremost negotiator and bargain hunter. After she bargains the big name retailer down as far as possible, she then offers to buy two of the item and re-quests an additional price reduction.

Retailers are faced with a dilemma. They can discount the item as low as possible, but if a customer wants to buy two, the quandary is whether to give a further discount. Jyll advises that sometimes there is one last step after the negotiation ends.

The Price Is Right Plus

When consumers arrive at a price that is fair or within their budget, they halt at this juncture and do not continue the negotiation. But a clever tactic, called the "Horn of Plenty" or "Sweeten the Deal," will help you discover what other goodies the seller can provide. The technique works best with big-ticket items that come with postsale service agreements, or with personal contracts for services (e.g., gardeners, cleaning services).

Here is how it works: Assume that the seller wants to close the deal; after you agree on the price, then demand other goodies before signing the contract. The first step is to make a list of all the items or services (e.g., spare parts, inspections) that define or can supplement your purchase.

Once you have outlined all the extras, then begin the negotiation. Let us imagine the purchase is a central air conditioning system for a house. The total price will include the purchase and the installation. But the store can deliver many other Horn of Plenty items. Assume it guarantees two free inspections during the first year and recommends one fully paid inspection the second. Ask for three free inspections the first year and 50 percent off the full price for the second year. Maybe the store will agree to one or both. What else is in the Horn of Plenty? What about a lower price for filters? What else? Ask an open-ended question: "What can you do to sweeten the deal?"

In a service agreement, the gardener may offer to come from spring to fall to perform the tasks outlined. But what about not just collecting the fall leaves but removing them? Ask for a discounted price on "x" number of new trees or bushes. Keep looking in the Horn of Plenty for more free or reduced-price items.

This method succeeds only at the beginning of a negotiation. The seller wants to close the deal and will accede to some of your requests. Be sure to put everything in writing.

Negotiable Opportunities Are Where You Find Them

A lawyer friend represented a senior executive at a large media company in the negotiation of his employment contract. The man became second in charge, and he and the CEO combined to make a successful team. The executive made the CEO godfather to his son, and the two families shared holidays and vacations together.

For years the business prospered, but then it fell into bad times. The CEO canned his second in command, and the terminated executive could not find another position. His life spiraled into debt and depression. It took a year for him to find another job at a lesser pay scale.

Cut to: FAO Schwarz, the wonderful toy store on Fifth Avenue, at Christmas time. The discharged executive and his son were shopping and ran into the CEO, whom they had not seen since the firing. The two men acted with cordial civility, but the son behaved in a cool and frosty manner. The CEO cum godfather said to the boy, "My Christmas gift to you is to pick out toys in the store for $100."

"Thank you, but I cannot accept," the boy answered.

"Why not?" asked the CEO.

"Because you didn't treat my Daddy nicely."

Without skipping a beat, the CEO said, "Make that $200 worth of toys."

Guilt, like everything else, is negotiable.

Dealing with Opponents

Negotiation is a one-to-one process, much like a chess game with an opening, a middle game, and an end game. It succeeds when two people are involved in a reasonable and flexible give-and-take. Negotiation does not do as well in a large group or communal procedure; think of it as too many cooks spoiling the settlement broth.

No one can state when it is the right moment to go for the jugular. I have learned that by looking into my opponent's eyes for a subtle clue, I will know when to put the dagger in. On some occasions, I can smell the fear.

When I sit down for a settlement conference with the other side, I begin by saying: "I am not in business to extort you, and I couldn't care less about the fact you have unreported income or that you're supporting a mistress, or a boyfriend or girlfriend, whatever. I want to settle the matter." When I mention those personal points, I look at the person to see if I hit home on a matter of personal substance. If, yes, I will see a pronounced reaction in the eyes, the muscles in the face, or the movement of the hands. Learn to spot these signs of anxiety as an advantage.

Julie Budd is a singer of immense talent, a former opening act for Frank Sinatra in Las Vegas. She told me that when her career began, he offered valuable performing tips. He demonstrated how a performer on stage could follow the spotlight by feeling its warmth atop the head. As the spotlight moves, a singer can develop a sense for where the spot shifts and stay under the light. I tried it once on stage, and after a few minutes, I could feel the light on my head as I moved under it.

The spotlight story speaks a similar truth; when you perceive fear or other reactions from an adversary, you can feel it and then train yourself to move with it to attain the upper hand.

It is vital to know the psychological makeup of the opposition, whether the person is a spouse, child, or a legal opponent. Some of this knowledge may come from past negotiation experience with this individual. Sometimes I remember familiar dialogue or recall past ploys. It is like facing a professional league baseball pitcher; if the curveball has been his most successful pitch, then it would be smart to look for it, or smarter yet, to avoid it.

WHEN TO GO FOR BROKE

Robert Evans, the film producer, said, "The only way you can make a deal is if you're ready to blow it."

I have an apartment in Florida along with a beach cabana. Instead of hanging a framed store-bought painting on one wall of my cabana, I wanted to have a mural painted of an idyllic tropical scene like palm trees or blue lagoons. I contacted a talented Cuban-American artist who sent me beautiful miniature mural samples with a price range from $2,200 to $4,200. (Whenever anyone says the price is "from . . . to," it is always the higher sum that will be charged.)

The mural was a spur-of-the-moment, half-thought-out idea; but on reflection, I discarded the notion and told the artist that although his work was beautiful, I would pass. Two weeks later, I received an e-mail from him stating that he would like to paint the mural. I replied that the top price in my budget was $1,000 and his fees were out of my range.

The artist responded that he could do a smaller wall painting for about $1,100. The point is, I had been ready to kill the deal since I was not convinced a mural was the right decorative choice. But when the price dropped dramatically, it ended my resistance and today I look at a beautiful mural.

Deliver What You Say

In an old FBI manual, I spotted a sentence that stated agents should draw a weapon only if they were prepared to use it. The premise holds for unions that threaten to strike if demands are not met: Unless the union is willing to go out on strike for a long time, the threat is useless. An important piece of advice is that once you agree on a decision, then deliver what you promised.

In a divorce case, when major disputes are settled, the parties are so delighted to be done that they will often leave one or two items open. An immutable fact is that saying these items will be worked out later means these dangling points will be talked over for a long time. Whatever is left open and unresolved at the settlement will give headaches in the future.

When signing a contractual agreement, the mechanisms must be in place to decide remaining items. If I negotiate an employment contract but omit the overtime provision, I am making a mistake, believing that it can be worked out at a later time. If, as in this case, overtime is left open in the agreement, there must be a system that states *exactly* how to deal with overtime in the future.

During a recent divorce case, the attorneys arrived at a settlement in principle and the papers were to be signed the next time the case appeared on the calendar for trial. I knew that the other lawyer had a reputation for negotiating a final agreement and then asking for revisions favorable to his client at the last minute. To combat this trick, I had 30 boxes of discovery material delivered to the courtroom where we would sign the final papers. The boxes were stacked up behind me to the ceiling, indicating that I was prepared to start the trial.

When my adversary entered the room, he stared at the 30 boxes. I said: "I am ready to sign the final papers as we agreed to. If you so much as offer one amendment to the case, I shall go to trial. I'll be back in a few minutes and I want a decision then." Being alone in the room, with nothing to look at but the weight of our case, convinced him to sign the papers. The stack of boxes represented the pistol I took out of my holster. I was prepared to go to trial, which I knew he wanted to avoid.

A Runaround with the Runyons

Damon Runyon was a revered American journalist, a talented sports writer who also covered notorious criminal trials such as the Lindbergh kidnapping. Today, with memories of old New York newspapers and nightclubs long forgotten, people often hear his name in connection with his short story "The Idyll of Miss Sarah Brown," which was adapted into the Broadway musical and movie *Guys and Dolls*.

Runyon was the ultimate chronicler of the show business, sports, and the gangster demimonde of New York City. He wrote a famous line that goes, "Long ago I came to the conclusion that all life is 6 to 5 against." Ironically, he was born in Manhattan, Kansas. His body was cremated, and his close friend, Eddie Rickenbacker, then the president of American Airlines, took the funeral urn on a small plane. He flew low over Manhattan, sprinkling the columnist's ashes over Times Square in a final tribute.

Runyon's son, Damon Junior, was a great friend of mine. Junior was also a newspaperman but remained in the shadow of his famous father's reputation. At one point, he was editor of "Focus," a daily column on the front page of the *New York Herald Tribune*. For a long time, Junior was an alcoholic, but in later years, he went on the wagon. A sad fact is that he ended his life by committing suicide.

Late one night, I received a call from Junior, who wanted to meet with me pronto. Since I am an insomniac, I had no problem getting dressed and meeting him at an all-night coffee shop. He confessed that 6 months earlier he had made a stupid blunder: While drunk, Junior had given a large trunk to a prostitute pal named Tall Tillie, one of his late-night bar companions. When he became sober, he recalled that his famous father had filled the trunk with manuscripts—unpublished works of literary significance, including short stories and a book—all of which represented large sums of money.

Junior's problem was that when he had asked Tall Tillie to give him back the trunk, she told him to buzz off. He asked me to negotiate an arrangement so that she would return the trunk with its literary contents. He trusted me and knew that I would not use any foul language. Tillie, her profession notwithstanding, could not tolerate profanity and speaking it around her (as Junior had done) precipitated a stern lecture to the speaker and then a slammed-down receiver or swift exit.

At his request, I called Tillie and arranged an early-morning rendezvous in a coffee shop after her business hours. I offered money for the trunk, emphasizing that it contained some of Junior's personal effects of a sentimental nature. She was not interested in Junior or his trunk, and then I said that he might pay $1,000. At first, she was taken aback by that sum of money but quickly deduced that the items in the trunk might have more than sentimental value and shrewdly bargained me up to $10,000. The trunk was worth this kind of money because Damon Runyon's writings inside could have been worth $1 million or more.

We made a deal. Then I tried to arrange the transfer of $10,000 for the trunk but she kept stalling on the delivery. At one point, I asked if she was trying to shake us down for more cash. But, as it turned out, she was unable to deliver the trunk because she had lost her temper and sold the trunk to a used furniture store for $25.00 after Junior cursed at her. During the months after we made the deal, she tried to determine what had happened to the trunk. She traced it to the store owner who remembered it was filled with musty and old yellow papers that he threw out in the garbage.

The moral is not to give hookers old trunks unless you first look inside. The cleverest negotiator may not be able to redress the bad consequences that result from your own foolish transaction.

Finding the Right Words

The right vocabulary is fundamental to negotiations. My experience is that "reasonable" and "flexible" are the two key words to begin settling a dispute. When a person says, "I know you are reasonable and flexible" at the outset of a negotiation process, it obligates the other side to a fair code of conduct. These words also set the tone for a civilized discussion.

Negative or challenging words achieve the opposite result; They will raise the hackles of an opponent and sabotage the procedure. The worst opening move is to force an adversary's back to the wall. Leave room for maneuver.

Final Thought

In negotiations, it is important to gauge the likely consequences of the outcome even if it produces a success. If I do not achieve the maximum for my client (but the settlement is fair), I may brood for a while but my life goes on. But if you go toe to toe with your spouse, child, or boss in a knock-down-drag-out fight and win, the consequences may mean the loss or damage of that relationship.

In this book, we will walk through some of life's minefields. If you pay close attention to my examples, you will wind up alive and healthy, and you will wear a smile of success.

2

DISTRACTIONS

Think of distraction as the conjurer's art: It is the "now you see it, now you don't" diversion that allows the magician to pull a quarter from a child's ear. In negotiations, it is the subtle practice of keeping your opponents' eyes on one object, while you hoodwink them with another.

T. S. Eliot, commenting about the way he wrote criticism, said words to this effect, "I am like the burglar who throws the dog a bone to go in the back door." The guard dog will drop the threatening pose and stop barking when the burglar rewards him with a delicious distraction. Bone throwing lures adversaries into unpromising positions, sending them to places they otherwise would not choose to go.

A fundamental application for a quick distraction is to offer time to think. On occasion, you may need an extra second to mull over a point or that extra minute to gather in thoughts. Create a pause to delay whatever is in process. Drop a file on the floor. Take a bathroom break. Signal a secretary to interrupt with an urgent telephone call. Do something, but do it quickly.

Varieties of Distractions

I can define three kinds of distractions: the personal, the semiprofessional, and the professional. All work, and each one can break up an adversary's measured pace during a meeting.

The personal distraction injects some familiarity into the conversation. Derail opponents by asking about their children or spouses. Sports fans will willingly detour from negotiation talks after you make inquiries about the past weekend's golf score or tennis game, or ask questions about the local college or professional sports teams. Or it could be a query about a particular cultural or political activity. Just make the question personal and sincere.

The semiprofessional distraction succeeds when bringing up a situation similar to the crux of the negotiation, whether it is a personal event or a business example. The approach allows taking a tangential line from a familiar event in the past to make a current point. I might use this in my practice by saying, "Isn't this similar to the appeal in the *Wasserman versus Rabinowitz* canine custody case?" In personal situations, it could be something akin to, "Aren't these vacation plans similar to last year when the entire family contracted poison ivy at Cornwall Bridge?" With these innocent reminders of earlier cases or situations, the direction of the negotiation moves off course and heads down a different trail (one that should be to your advantage).

The professional diversion goes deep into the heart of the case. "What's on the table?" you ask in the midst of the discussion. This seems like a direct and forthright approach, but in fact it is a gambit that allows you to disguise the key issue. Labor negotiations serve as a good example. On the table are wages, hours, vacations, health benefits, and other standard negotiation objectives. But assume that the most important point is keeping out a union shop. By dropping the topic of the union shop into the same grab bag of negotiable issues, you can insert into the debate without provocation.

I learned the art of the credible diversion from a businessman who had an office on the floor above mine when I first started in private practice. He dressed elegantly in double-breasted British suits, regimental rep ties, and monogrammed, handmade shirts. He was a sales representative for prestigious metropolitan cemeteries, and his job was to presell plots to wealthy, prominent WASP Manhattan families.

To meet prospective new clientele, he joined New York's most elite social clubs. He knew from past experience that at the committee meetings of these clubs, the men would go around the table, stand up, and introduce themselves by giving name, prep school, and college. On any given occasion, one might hear, "Patrick Clarkson. Bolles. Princeton." And other members would say, "Yes, Bolles. Princeton. First-rate." The next fellow would say, "Chris Rhodes. Hotchkiss. Yale." And the crowd would repeat, "Yes. Hotchkiss. Yale. First-rate."

When the sales rep stood up—looking more stylishly dressed than anyone else in the room—he would say with pronounced authority, "Jim Shrock, Adams. Worsham." A slight pause followed, but then the men said, "Yes. Adams. Worsham. First-rate." After the meeting, some of the more curious members would approach and ask, "Isn't Worsham a small, private college?" He would reply, "Yes, it's located in Illinois and only graduates a select class each year." "First-rate," echoed the members, pleased to welcome Shrock as the right kind of person into their social circle.

What Shrock did not reveal was that Adams stood for John Adams High School and Worsham was a mortuary college. His sleight of hand had succeeded. His looks, apparent breeding, and the obscurity of his alma mater provided the distraction that curtailed further inquiry into his plebian background.

When one enters an office, the furniture and other accoutrements contain a message about the person. The room speaks before the speaking begins. In my office, I have various diplomas on the wall including an honorary degree from Oxford University, England. I have pictures autographed by U.S. presidents, other political dignitaries, and J. Edgar Hoover. I have a Picasso oil that I obtained from Claude Picasso, a Rouault painting, a Henry Moore piece, and a bust by Rodin. Before I say a word, the lineup on the wall has said volumes about me as a person who can be trusted. If negotiation takes place in my office, I have already established my credibility.

Explanations Not

In your professional and personal life, you will encounter the chronic explainers who want to impress you with detailed research and scholarly raison d'être for having arrived at a certain position. They have spent hours—sometimes, even days—calculating and refiguring the variables to reach a conclusion. Their goal is to sway your opinion by citing chapter and verse using this tedious method.

When I sense my adversary has a lengthy explanation waiting in the wings and wants to introduce it into the negotiations, I say, "Assuming everything you will tell me is correct, I am not interested. I think we should head to the bottom line." If the opposition still persists in going further, I call up the scene in A. Conan Doyle's, *The Final Problem*, when Professor Moriarty at last meets Sherlock Holmes and says, "You evidently don't know me." Holmes replies, "On the contrary, I think it is fairly evident that I do. Pray take a chair. I can spare you five minutes if you have anything to say." Moriarty again, "All that I have to say has already crossed your mind." Holmes, "Then possibly my answer has crossed yours." And all that my pedantic opponents have to say has already crossed mine.

GETTING TO THERE

Adversaries often begin with some boring background piece about the history of the controversy or whatever brought the negotiation to the table. I make it clear that I am not interested in past circumstances. My sole concern is not how we got here, but rather how do we get out of here?

My sudden and impromptu interruption has two main goals; the first is to stifle opponents from spouting a prepared spiel ad nauseum. They have lived for this moment and are convinced that after I listen to the weight of their arguments, I will bend like the proverbial reed in the wind. The second reason, which almost always accompanies the first, is that a settlement figure will represent their bottom line. But this number is not *my* bottom line and I do not care at all how brilliantly they calculated the amount.

Another lesson I have learned is that it is very difficult to convince another person to move to your position. Most people will neither relinquish nor change preconceived ideas; often, they are too frightened or insecure to move off a point. Therefore, attempting to reason with somebody on a logical basis does not work. People will change on the basis of self-interest; they will be flexible if they want to achieve a certain goal. But individuals convinced of the inherent rightness of their position will never retreat. The most that you can accomplish is a financial negotiation to increase the size of a settlement. The legitimacy of their argument has not been challenged, only the sum.

DATA NOT

Hypothetically, the other attorneys in a divorce case have reviewed precedence and other factors to arrive at the sum of $1 million. Maybe the path that led them to this number would fill a large spreadsheet, and accountants and other lawyers would heap praise for its inspired mathematical rationale. But I have a target number for my client of $2 million. I refuse to be sucked into the whirlpool of their rationale; I want to obtain the maximum. If I play the game of reviewing the settlement to refute their numbers point by point, I will lose the argument.

For example, when divorce lawyers review the value of a medical practice, they want to explain how they used industry charts to reflect that my physician client earns more than the norm. But if I have in my mind that the value of the practice is $120,000, as opposed to the adversary's formula of $200,000, I cannot play the game of excess earnings because I will go down to defeat. My opponent has detailed values for each variable of the practice, including the doctor's age, specialty, and status. I indicate to my adversaries the road has to end up in Mecca, and Mecca is where I say it is, not what appears on a spreadsheet.

THIRD-PARTY DISTRACTIONS

When I prepare for a case, I am like an army general who organizes three possible attack strategies. I have my "A" or main plan; but I also have a "B" fallback strategy and a "C" tactic, or a last-ditch, bailout plan. The A strategy and its relevant points represent the meaty thrust of the argument's main line.

From time to time, I have to present a client's position to a third-party arbitrator. As much as I object to this method, there are occasions when another person (judge, facilitator, mediator, family friend, or relative) can offer a distraction that will prove a boon to my argument. Assume I am deep into the facts of the A plan, and out of the blue, the judge asks a question that has nothing to do with my prepared reasoning but may be a minor point in the C strategy. Here is the unforeseen diversion that may tip the scales of the decision my way. The arbitrator has focused on a point that may help determine the outcome of the case. It does not matter whether I concur, I have to seize on the new remark and run with it.

In cases argued in the U.S. Supreme Court, the justices interrupt repeatedly to ask questions of the attorneys presenting. These explorations give court experts a clue into what the particular justice thinks about the case. The queries are distractions indicating the areas of resistance that the lawyer will have to overcome to win that justice's endorsement.

A well-prepared lawyer can twist these questions around and adjust ready-made answers (perhaps part of a B or C plan) so that they become suitable responses to the arbitrator or judge.

A comedian comes on the Jay Leno Show. Leno asks him a question. The comedian has set jokes and he is able to twist the question around so he can answer with a prepared and tested comeback. We also see this behavior with politicians. On the stump, they use a set speech that they repeat often during the campaign. They come to a town hall meeting, or even a television press conference, and someone asks a question. These politicians rephrase it so that they can use the rehearsed, "on message" stump speech and frequently do not really address the question asked.

The idea is never to let anybody in a negotiation or any similar situation take you to an unknown or unfamiliar place. Never go down a road unless you know where it leads. Maintaining control is essential, and any detour should be a very short one.

No Ticket

Life also throws some distractions that can be helpful in many situations.

I was Rudy Giuliani's attorney in his divorce proceedings, the details of which remain confidential. He and I had many conversations on different topics before the case and we continued to talk after it was settled. After the tragic events of September 11, 2001, he was knighted by the Queen of England and chosen as

Time magazine's "Person of the Year." His name would be recognized by almost all Americans, and his face and voice by almost everyone in the New York metropolitan area and perhaps beyond.

Guiliani is a 24-hours-a-day person who could wear out teams of colleagues and assistants with his nonstop energy. Toward the end of 1995 (when he was mayor of New York), I was driving out to Long Island when the telephone rang in my car. I pulled over, knowing that my office would not patch through a call unless it was important. There was no shoulder on the road so instead I turned down a private lane that seemed to be the entryway into a vineyard. I could not have parked more than 10 yards on the private lane.

The telephone call was from the mayor, and after the conversation had continued for about 15 minutes, a Suffolk County Sheriff's car drove up behind me. The trooper approached me cautiously. The people in the main house on the vineyard estate must have become suspicious about a strange car parked for such a long time on their private road. The trooper signaled me to climb out of the car, but my mind was elsewhere. I was deep in conversation with the mayor and did not comply with the policeman's order. Without thinking, I shooed the trooper away with a wave of my hand. My refusal to hang up irritated him (for good reason), and he then demanded to see my license and registration.

Annoyed, I said, "Just wait, can't you see I'm on the telephone?"

"What?"

"I am talking to the mayor of New York, and you will just have to wait."

He regarded me curiously. Was I a nutcase?

I ignored him and continued speaking, turning away so he could not hear the conversation. He was uncertain what to do but apparently decided I must be on the level, since who would be crazy enough to ignore a police officer with an outrageous story about talking to the mayor of New York City? When the telephone conversation ended, I exited the car to respond to his inquiry.

One Fourth of July years ago, the late British press magnate Robert Maxwell invited me to view Macy's spectacular Independence Day fireworks aboard the four-masted barque *Peking*, which was docked at the Seaport in Manhattan as a tourist attraction. He was the head of the Mirror Group Newspapers, which at one time owned several London newspapers, Permagon Press, and 50 percent of MTV in Europe. He was an over-the-top narcissist who also owned the *New York Daily News* for a short while. He loved to entertain and that July evening we were treated to a sumptuous buffet, the sounds of bagpipers from England, and the wonderful young voices of the All-City Choir.

After the fireworks, a group of us, including the then Bronx Borough President Freddy Ferrer and also CBS's Walter Cronkite, disembarked and searched for taxis to take us uptown. But the police had blocked off the entire Lower East Side of Manhattan to accommodate the enormous holiday crowd. There was no surface traffic except for police and sanitation vehicles.

When we reached First Avenue, a police captain recognized Ferrer, who explained our transportation predicament. The officer stopped an empty city bus that had wandered into the area and ordered it to turn north. We piled in, including others in the crowd and one pregnant woman, the choral director of the All-City Choir. She appeared distraught and I asked why. She replied that her husband in Brooklyn would be worried that he had not heard from her after the fireworks.

I handed her my cell phone (cell phones at that time were just coming into use). The woman dialed her husband who was concerned she was heading north in Manhattan instead of taking a subway home to Brooklyn. She tried to allay his apprehension by saying, "I'm fine. I'm fine. I'm sitting next to Walter Cronkite." Then her expression turned sour. "He hung up on me," she said.

"He told me to stop the Cronkite nonsense and come home. I guess he thought I was drunk."

Cronkite said, "Call again and I'll speak to him. What are your names?"

"Anne and Bob," she replied and redialed the number. "Honey, I am going to put Walter Cronkite on," she said, handing the former CBS anchor the telephone.

And in that deep, rumbling, unmistakable, and familiar voice, Cronkite said, "Hello, Bob, Anne is in good hands and she'll be home soon. We enjoyed a wonderful time, watching the fireworks. And that's the way it was, July Fourth, the nation's birthday. This is Walter Cronkite saying good night." The husband relaxed at once.

MAKE IT PERSONAL

During a recent conference, I found myself in the offices of an opposing law firm with which I had negotiated for 35 years. I knew the senior partners, most of whom I had met in legal and social situations. Because of our schedules, we had allotted only a half-hour for the settlement meeting. The presentation assignment was given to a young associate. I did not want to be bogged down, listening to a youthful attorney's well-rehearsed patter. So, I began reminiscing with the other lawyers in the conference room. Back and forth we went, swapping war stories about the good old days and commiserating about the changes for the worse in the legal field. I could see that this distraction was causing the young lawyer discomfort as the time ticked away and I continued harking back to days of long ago. Because of his junior position in the firm, the young man had to listen in respectful silence.

With the sand in the hourglass running out, I said to the young lawyer, "We have limited time. I am sure you have a great presentation but, please, give me the bottom line number?" He told me what it was. "Unacceptable," I replied and exited the conference room, shaking the other lawyers' hands and commenting how enjoyable it had been to remember old friends and old memories. The subtext of the meeting was that I was interested solely in the bottom line and the rest represented window dressing. The next day, the offer was raised without the necessity of having to listen to the long explanation behind the unimpressive settlement.

When lawyers want to justify the number or explain why justice rests on their side, I repeat Lenny Bruce's comment, "If you want to find justice in the halls of justice, look in the halls." I explain that justice is not a commodity with which I can deal. I can deal with flexible solutions to reasonable problems. While the presentation would be of interest and make nice music, the lyrics are my sole concern.

Making Your Case

I never want to travel down the precedence case route introduced by my opposition because it represents an obvious trap. I am in trouble unless I can cite a contradictory decision to counter the cases (difficult but not impossible while debating on the spot). Too many people in my profession love their own legal double-talk or "lawyerspeak" and will cite cases and decisions ad infinitum.

With erudite attorneys, once in a while, I will counter with a fictitious case. On a few occasions, I have used these nonexistent cases as distractions to break up opponents' rhythms and put them at a disadvantage. When I hear the other lawyer say, "Let's remember what happened in *Brisk v. Fox* when Judge Gross ruled . . . " I may reply, *"Brisk v. Fox* doesn't apply in this situation, but *Lewis v. South Carolina* does." And, of course, *Lewis v. South Carolina* is invention.

Often, the other lawyer will nod and say, "Quite right, *Lewis v. South Carolina* may be on point, but. . . . " I have known a few lawyers who used fictitious cases in front of judges, but this is not a tactic I would recommend with people of authority who will decide the fate of the negotiations.

Some years ago, I tried a case before Hortense Gable, an elderly judge in the twilight of her career. My client took the stand and testified to her husband's conversations and also to his threats. The other attorney cited a particular section of the law that predictably said what every viewer of TV crime programs knows: A wife cannot testify against a husband. This lawyer said that this section also included actions that the husband *did* to the wife. The statements surprised us, but the judge did not have the applicable law in the courtroom. She directed an assistant to find the statute, located in another room of the courthouse, and bring it back for examination. The clerk returned in 15 minutes, and the judge read the section but discovered no exception to the rule. She glowered at the lawyer, and if torture had been available to her, his body would have been stretched out on the rack. The moral: Before citing cases that do not exist, lawyers should make sure the judge will not spend the time to determine their bona fides.

THE VALUE OF DISTRACTIONS

Distractions add imponderables to the discussion. The more balls you keep in the air, the more you have to play with. A well-executed distraction will divert opponents from their game plan.

 **3**

NEVER WANT
TOO MUCH

Years ago, Sol Goldman was the largest real estate owner in New York other than the Archdiocese of New York and the city itself. An unassuming person, he owned more than 800 buildings when he died. I represented him in a contentious divorce that terminated in 1987. At one point, I asked him how he had accumulated such enormous wealth. He replied, "I never wanted anything so much that I couldn't walk away from it."

In negotiations, as in life, if you want something too much, you will pay too big a financial or psychological price because you will act on your emotions and not on your goal. You will end up on the losing end.

In some divorce cases, people come into my office hoping to get even with the spouse for an alleged emotional injury. They are out for revenge; they want to humiliate and punish the other person—and they want the world to know about it. Often, I hear an impassioned new client (in general, but not exclusively, a woman) say, "I want you to carve up that SOB into little pieces. I want his reputation dragged through the mud. I want our children and our friends to know what a scoundrel he is and how terribly he treated me." I am going to have trouble with this client because divorce is not about squaring accounts; it is not about settling scores; and it is not about righting a moral wrong in the universe. Divorce is about negotiation.

Despite the new no-fault divorce system, some clients continue to hire lawyers to be an instrument of revenge. These people are not interested in simply obtaining the most money from a settlement but want to adopt a scorched-earth, take-no-prisoners policy. Some of them believe they are entitled to reparations, and if I defer to their wish, I may not be able to move the case toward a fair settlement or even one tipped in our favor. There are men and women who want to air dirty linen. They would take pleasure in embarrassing, disgracing, and even forcing a final twilight of the Gods, a Götterdämmerung that could destroy both parties in the process. My objective is to make the best settlement.

A lawyer assumes a variety of personae for different clients, and changes character at different points of time, even as the law changes. When I started practicing law, clients viewed their lawyer as a white knight, charging forth on a stallion to rescue them. Now the pendulum has swung the other way, and with the advent of no-fault divorce, a lawyer is often perceived as a routine but necessary instrument of the legal system. We are relegated to a dull role somewhere between an accountant and an appraiser, whose sole function is to sit with another lawyer to divide up assets evenly.

John Gibson of Fox News, one of the country's preeminent television legal reporters, did outstanding commentary during the O. J. Simpson case. One day, after the termination of the Giuliani divorce case (I represented the ex-mayor against his then wife Donna Hanover), Gibson and I bumped into each other at NBC. For the record, I have always honored the legal confidentiality in my cases. I followed these legal rules with Gibson when he inquired about the Giuliani divorce.

I told him straightforwardly that I could not talk about the case. He respected my wishes, but a few minutes later (tenacious journalist that he is), he took me aside and said, "Okay, I know you cannot and will not talk about the case, but tell me if I am wrong: Donna Hanover's lawyers claimed a 'tremendous victory.' But if people look at the publicized settlement numbers, how could it be a victory?"

Gibson was recalling newspaper stories that had quoted Hanover's attorneys, who gave a detailed breakdown of Guiliani's anticipated finances. The press printed her financial demands, which they obtained from court papers or from her attorneys. When Hanover's lawyer trumpeted those statements to the press, that attorney had the benefit of having seen the disclosure on the mayor's finances. Gibson again pressed me for information, saying: "Hanover may have succeeded in making the public believe the result was tremendously favorable to her. But from what I recollect of the dollar figures already published and her demands, it seemed she obtained a poor result." I responded by telling him to have a good day, and we both smiled and went our separate ways. I never answered the question.

A year after the Giuliani divorce was concluded, I shook my head in sad reflection of human behavior and the happiness of people. I had just read news accounts of Hanover's press agent calling newspapers and magazines in a desperate attempt for media coverage of the announcement of her engagement, which took place on the sidewalk outside Tiffany's with the two Giuliani children present. At least one major newspaper mocked Hanover, perhaps with the memory of her oft-repeated position that she considered herself a private homebody who had always wanted to avoid the limelight and, above all, shield the children from the media.

Let me segue to a 1948 film *The Saxon Charm;* Robert Montgomery played an unscrupulous, media-hungry Broadway producer who some believed was patterned after David Merrick. Another actor in the film said of Montgomery's oily character, "If he had the choice of sleeping with a woman and no one knowing, or not sleeping with her, and everyone thinking he went to bed with her, he would choose the latter over the former."

As I walked away from John Gibson, the comment in *The Saxon Charm* danced in my head. Did Donna Hanover sacrifice a better settlement for one gratifying moment of hearing an almost hysterical outcry from her lawyer broadcast a "tremendous victory" on the courthouse steps? History may one day tell this tale. I never shall.

Paying for Privacy Never Pays

It is difficult to keep scandal out of the press. Ask former Colorado Senator Gary Hart, who denied any extramarital affair, and told the media to follow him if they doubted his integrity. That is precisely what the *Miami Herald* did and caught him snuggling Donna Rice on a pleasure boat named, ironically, *Monkey Business.* I can state with certainty that if intrepid journalists start to dig into the lives of celebrities, sooner or later, they will come up with some juicy morsel. Or, if a spouse is clever at leaking information, the tittle-tattle will make its way circuitously through friends of friends to the media. A wag once said that gossip is the abandoned baby left anonymously on the doorstep of the press.

When the public views a front-page look at the scandal, the outraged party who demanded confidentiality can scream that the agreement has been breached. But proving it can become a difficult and fruitless task. The substantial sums paid to guard privacy have been thrown away for nothing. These clauses may work if monies for confidentiality are doled out monthly over a two- or three-year period. After that, the story has died and been buried, and few care what happened to whom back when.

Privacy is a realm that people want too much. In cases of divorce or paternity suits, when one party asks for and receives a confidentiality agreement, it is an example of paying for nothing. As a matter of law, these are foolish clauses to insert into a settlement because enforcement is difficult.

Think back to the odyssey of Jack Welch, perhaps the most famous CEO in the United States during the past 20 years. Welch took the helm at General Electric and significantly increased its revenues and assets. He then wrote a best-selling book, explaining his methodologies for business success. But after retirement, he became embroiled in a very public and angry divorce case with his estranged second wife. She announced to the press that the reason for the divorce was her husband's affair with the editor of the *Harvard Business Review,* whom he had met during an interview. He retaliated with charges that she had also taken a lover.

Striking out in public against her husband, the bruised Mrs. Welch revealed much of her husband's finances to the public. He had received many perks from General Electric, including an expensive apartment, transportation, and club membership as part of his generous retirement package. Since Welch had been the golden boy executive at General Electric and had raised the value of the company's stock, he could have asked for any perquisite he wanted. If a vote had been taken of the shareholders—even assuming they knew about the high financial cost of his retirement to General Electric—they probably would have voted for the generous package with eagerly raised arms. On the other hand, some naysayers voiced a contrary opinion, saying, in effect, "Welch had been compensated an enormous amount of money as salary each year to produce results. If he had not generated profits, would we then have requested he return part of his income?"

General Electric came to an agreement with Welch, who voluntarily returned some of the perks after the shocking size of the retirement package became public. Here is the irony in this case; by returning some of the retirement benefits, he lowered his net worth and also his available income. Indeed, stretching the example, Jack Welch could claim that his ex-wife was the cause of the dissipation (the forced relinquishment) of retirement assets. He could try to insist on an economic benefit flowing from her to him in the divorce. The net effect was that the marital pie was now smaller and Mrs. Welch would receive less because of her vengeful actions of going public with her husband's retirement package.

The Connecticut judge in the Welch case sealed the files, denying the transcript to the media. In view of the First Amendment, the sealed files could not be made public, but the court's action would not stop either of the Welches from giving interviews to the press to bolster their own case. Nor would it stop the press from attending and reporting on future court proceedings. The judge signed an additional order prohibiting both parties from revealing the business aspects of the case. Of course, the couple still could discuss the personal characteristics of one another or the dynamics of their failed marriage.

The judge's ruling may work fine for Jack Welch, but it is somewhat questionable whether it will survive appellate review. Most of the time, judges have been upheld on gag order rulings when the spouses have young children who may be hurt by the publicity. In the case of the Welches, no young children were involved and the court did not have to worry about bruising sensitive and innocent psyches.

In the final analysis, I suppose that neither of the Welches would want to appeal the ruling because it would indicate that they indeed had intended to use the press for their own purposes. Keeping the dirty laundry a secret could have a positive effect on family harmony. I am convinced, however, that these gag order clauses are not worth negotiating, either in time or money spent, since matters tend to be made public one way or another.

HEAVYWEIGHTS

I represented actress Robin Givens in a divorce case against heavyweight boxer, Mike Tyson. Few people knew that an expensive and controlled public relations machine sanitized his reputation. From the earliest days of bare-knuckle champions, a glowing aura surrounded the heavyweight champions. In the end, Tyson diminished the historic glow.

Givens and her mother were vilified—falsely accused of drugging the champ. Robin's mother is a lovely woman who had positive remarks to say about Tyson and warmly considered him a son. Givens dropped out of Harvard Medical School at age 19, and perhaps this past medical association created the false idea that mother and daughter were slipping the champ Mickey Finns to render him a zombie.

The "evidence" for the drugging lie occurred when Tyson appeared in an ABC television "20/20" interview with Barbara Walters. To the viewing audience, he appeared in a semi-somnambulant state. Weeks later, the program released the video outtakes of Tyson before and after the interview, clearly showing that he was lively and in no way drugged. He apparently was ill at ease in front of the camera, but that did not stop the media from inventing malicious stories about Givens and her mother.

The stigma of being the person at fault in the divorce dogged Robin Givens for years afterward. The accusations stopped after Tyson was unmasked, revealing his dark character to the world. He ended up going to jail for rape and, after prison, further damaged his reputation with a bizarre biting-the-ear-in-the-ring episode as well as other subsequent weird events and televised statements.

In the play *Agamemnon*, the Greek Chorus shouts, "But good, prevail, prevail." Deservedly so, good has prevailed for Robin Givens.

FIRST OUT OF THE GATE

Sometimes people attempt to manipulate the media to assist their cause in a divorce or other unpleasant legal case. This is particularly true in a criminal case, where favorable public sentiment might affect the potential jury pool. In the Laci Peterson murder case, it appeared that Scott Peterson's representatives leaked information to the degree that the court issued a gag order.

It is the person with the more substantial press machine or money who feels that going to the media will provide a head start in bending public opinion. Press agents or public relations firms representing politicians agree that it is important to be the first one out of the gate to define the issues, because it forces adversaries to dance to that particular politician's tune.

In 1990, I represented Johnny Carson's first wife, Jody. At that time, the late-night host was one of the highest paid television celebrities in the world. Years after their divorce, she returned to court for relief, or in layperson's terminology, an increase in spousal support. To create a favorable image of Carson in the media, his lawyer stood in the court hallway after the first court appearance handing out to the press a printed guide explaining why Carson would prevail on the issues. The television star showed more interest in the court of public opinion than in the outcome of the courtroom.

Lawyers can misuse well-known personalities. I represented the wife of Al Roker, the NBC weatherman. She is a fine and elegant woman, and we took every step to respect her privacy. This divorce remained private at the beginning of negotiations. Then one day to my distress, I noticed an item by George Rush, a respected columnist in the *New York Daily News*, containing details about the Roker divorce. The tip-off for the columnist's source should have been that it spoke in complimentary terms of Roker's lawyer, who then was not well known in legal circles.

Roker was furious at the item and convinced that I had planted it. I was unhappy with the item and called Rush, who, as I anticipated and true to his profession, would not divulge the source. But I said, "George, one fact is certain, while I respect your code of confidentiality, we both know that I never gave you this item."

I then made an accusation in chambers in front of Judge Walter Schachman right to the face of Roker's attorney, who did not reply. His silence spoke volumes. At one point, I challenged this lawyer to a lie detector test, promising that if I lost, I would give to charity 10 dollars to every one of his dollars. He never accepted the wager.

Roker remains convinced to this day that I was the one who tipped the *Daily News*. Proof is that for years on his web site, I have been attacked in an ongoing diatribe that curses me for the newspaper's embarrassing story. Here's what he continues to rant about:

> Having gone through a bitter divorce a few years back, and having my ex-wife's sleaze ball lawyer, Raoul Felder try and drag my name through the mud, I am very sensitive to this subject. When all is said and done, all these cases of public figures and the exposing of the seamier side of their private lives boils down to money.

Roker should have expressed these negative feelings to his own lawyer. I did my best to keep his situation private, but maybe it makes Roker feel better to blame his wife's lawyer, even though I was not the bad guy.

Overeager press agents can influence public opinion in celebrity divorces. I represented David Guest in his split-up from Liza Minnelli. At the outset, the separation negotiations proceeded amicably and in private. But Minnelli's press agent leaked favorable stories about their client to the *National Enquirer* and the

New York Post. Once the divorce became public, *People* magazine interviewed the couple's friends—the result was that Liza's image was damaged and Guest appeared sympathetic.

Roy Cohen was one of the best-known lawyers in the United States. Before becoming a successful attorney in private practice, he had a career in government, culminating in serving as counsel on the notorious McCarthy Committee hearings in the 1950s. My observation was that, although Cohen was a bright perhaps even a brilliant individual, when we went to court, he was often unprepared. Clients represented a minor consideration, if not an annoyance to him. His main concern was volume, which generated large sums of money, and he was never concerned with the quality of his legal representation.

Cohen's lifetime goal was not to pay taxes although he earned a great deal of money. One time, IRS special agents came to my office and asked for copies of documents in a divorce case, which revealed the amount of fees Cohen had received from his client. I refused to give them the papers. Putting aside general personal principles, the contents of my files remained privileged by law unless waived by a client. The agents left my office chagrined, but they remembered later that the case had been appealed. The IRS visited the intermediate New York Appellate Court and obtained the papers they wanted, as any citizen could have done by filing a request. At that time, a loophole in the confidentiality statute permitted anyone to ask for papers from the Clerk's Office of the New York Court of Appeals. This marks another example in the past of how people could circumvent confidentiality.

I repeat my contention that confidentiality is never worth paying an extra penny.

DUBIOUS OVERPAYMENTS

A client of mine purchased the rights to buy the northeast corner building at Fifth Avenue and East Fifty-Seventh Street 20 years ago at a time when Japanese investors started to buy large parcels of New York City's prime real estate. The corner building was a two-story bank and later became, for a number of years, a Warner Brothers store.

When a building is purchased, initially a contract is drawn up, which is an agreement to buy the property for a stated price. About three months later after a title search to assure the buyer that he will receive "clean title," is when the actual closing takes place. At contract time, the prospective buyer puts down 10 percent of the value of the purchase price. This is the token that binds the deal and is forfeited to the seller should the buyer renege on the acquisition. When my client went to contract on this building, he never put down a penny as a deposit, let alone the required 10 percent. Since he was wealthy, he entered into an arrangement whereby he segregated the 10 percent in the bank by putting it into a sort of escrow account.

Japanese investors came knocking on my client's door after learning that the property was on the market. They offered to take over his contract to purchase the site and obtain the right to buy the building at the price he had negotiated. My client wanted to own the building and was disinterested in selling the contract. But the Japanese offered to give him almost $10 million above what he should have put as a down payment for the purchase if he would sell them the contract. He made the deal, losing the building but making $10 million quick profit and never spending or risking a penny.

My client's real estate lawyer asked the Japanese why they were so willing to enter into this expensive deal. They explained that they knew it was an overpayment but were willing to pay a high premium because, aside from obtaining a landmark building, it was an educational experience; they were learning how to deal in New York real estate. When the New York real estate bubble burst in the 1990s, they were forced to sell off their overpriced and overpaid properties at huge losses, including the purchase of Rockefeller Center. The idea of becoming landholders in Manhattan may have seemed attractive at the time, but it was not worth the eventual cost and loss of money and property. The Japanese wanted Manhattan too much and paid the price. That is the true lesson.

THE SINATRA SYNDROME

In 1953, Frank Sinatra convinced Hollywood film director Fred Zinnemann to let him star as Maggio in the film version of the novel *From Here to Eternity*. Sinatra coveted the role and agreed to a low fee, gambling that the part would boost his sagging career. And did it ever. He won an Oscar for Best Supporting Actor, and from that moment on, his stardom was ascendant. He regained lost status.

I have coined the phrase the "Sinatra Syndrome," to describe people who will stake their incomes to gain status. For example, a star newscaster in a small city market may agree to take a position in a major metro area for less money. The lure is the status of becoming a small fish in a big market. But for every one Sinatra success story, life narrates a hundred tales where the gamble did not produce success and the person incurred a real loss in wages. Seeking status was worth bubkes.

SPORT AGENTS' STRATEGY

Agents for professional athletes employ a shrewd bargaining tactic to maximize negotiations when they represent three or four athletes on the same team. They use the lowest price players as sacrificial lambs in bargaining sessions, knowing that the team will pay enormous sums for the superstars.

I am familiar with this tactic from my friendship with the late Bill Goodstein who was a lawyer-tenant in my offices. He was an avid sports fan, particularly of baseball, and his career goal was to become a player's agent. While driving home one night, he pulled up to another car at a red light. Sitting inside the other vehicle was baseball star Reggie Jackson, of the New York Yankees. He and Goodstein exchanged in small talk while their cars stood side by side; then they pulled over to a late-night coffee shop, where they had a long conversation about sports and sports agents.

This serendipitous meeting was the genesis of Goodstein becoming a sports agent. He became friendly with one of the bat-boys on the Yankees, a resident of the Dominican Republic, who could introduce him to Dominican and other Spanish-speaking players. Goodstein attempted to sign them up for his stable of athletes.

At one point, a newspaper quoted George Steinbrenner, who alluded to an anonymous sports agent lurking in the private parking lot at Yankee Stadium. That was Goodstein, and friends jokingly addressed him afterward as "The Lurker."

Goodstein represented several well-known ballplayers, including Willie Randolph and Dave Righetti, who pitched a no-hitter on his initial appearance with the Yankees. He also was able to sign up other less valuable players who, he explained, gave him bargaining maneuverability. In negotiations, Goodstein represented a mix of major and minor league players. He could throw in or take out the lesser players in a package deal. The minor talented players were the dispensable pawns in the bigger chess game of negotiating multimillion-dollar deals for the superstars.

One day, Goodstein opened the mail and extracted a book that arrived with a note from ex-President Richard Nixon, an avid baseball fan. Nixon wanted to send Dave Righetti a congratulatory note on the no-hitter and also an autographed book but did not know where to mail it, so he sent it to Goodstein. In the note, Nixon recounted other no-hitters he had seen and enjoyed.

This high and low strategy is a common negotiation practice for agents who deal with sports, show business, and even television newscaster contracts. Large theatrical talent agencies have honed it to perfection. A single agency representing all the talent sometimes puts together the entire creative side of a movie—writers, director, actors—balancing one against the other.

No House Divided

In the division of marital property, the wife will often—some divorce lawyers will say almost always—request the former marital house or apartment as part of the settlement. Wives will give irrational but heartfelt reasons to combat the financial logic that recommends the sale of the residence. The women often claim that to rent a home or apartment would cost more than maintaining the marital residence, which works with voodoo math but not in the real world.

The wives' reasoning overlooks the cost of money. If $500,000 is tied up in a residence, what follows is the income loss of the use of that money in terms of normalized interest rates. These sums could represent considerable monies. To this argument, wives turn a deaf ear. Instead, they protest, "I must keep the home for my kids when they come back home," even though the children may be living at boarding school or be fourty-five years old.

Another argument is that the residence is a valuable investment, which will increase in the future. This may be true if real estate keeps going up; but it also could go down (ask the Japanese). The reasoning is flawed because even if the house value appreciates, wives will continue to live in the residence and not sell it for possible profit.

We are all victims of Newton's law: Bodies at rest tend to stay at rest; bodies in motion tend to stay in motion. If a woman has resided in a home for many years, leaving it will be difficult for her. But if a woman has lived a gypsy life, always on the go, then moving will pose no problem, and she will be amenable to a sale of the house.

I have wasted hours with female clients, reviewing the arithmetic of the value of a residence to no avail. No matter how precise my mathematical presentation, wives will not see the financial benefit of selling the residence and dividing up the sale price with their husbands. I often suggest that women look at other houses or apartment alternatives in the same locale to learn firsthand that they can stay in the area in a smaller, less expensive residence. Then, they can pocket and bank the difference from the sale of the larger residence.

To hold onto an apartment or house, divorced women may try to throw monkey wrenches that could impede or prevent the sale of the property. They will cancel real estate appointments with brokers or never show the house to potential buyers. If the real estate broker arrives for an appointment, the door will be locked. To discourage would-be buyers, wives often make the house look neglected, messy, and unattractive. I had one case where a wife "innocently" mentioned to a prospective purchaser, "There must be a curse in this house; two people died horribly in that bedroom."

To prevent wives from engaging in these destructive tactics, I am specific about contractual points relating to the sale subsequent to the divorce agreement. We stipulate the price to be asked, timetable for property transfer, and when personal property and furniture will be removed. Nothing is left for later discussions.

Often an ex-wife faces dire economic consequences when she insists on keeping the residence. The woman ends the divorce with the thought, "Give me just six months in the house, and then I'll sell it." Then it becomes, "Give me just a year in the house, and then I'll sell it." Then time passes, and it becomes two years or four years or whenever. But in maintaining the home, she is like the person standing in front of the slot machine who keeps tossing coins, saying, "I'll spend another ten dollars," which becomes another ten dollars and another ten after that.

Financial reality dictates the quick disposal of the residence after the divorce. But wives who want security or stability too much overpay for that privilege.

THE HIGH COST OF STATUS

For better or for worse, I am a public figure (although not in the same recognizable media category as Harrison Ford or Joe Torre). Nevertheless, in the legal sense I am a public person, my notoriety stemming from numerous media interviews and appearances on television and published articles (many with my photograph) in newspapers and magazines.

One of the few benefits of status, of being recognized by the public (aside from having to overtip everywhere), is that most people will take my phone calls and also will feel free to call me, even if we have never met. I have taken phone calls from European royalty and from Paul Newman and other celebrities.

I remember my office routing a phone call from Jay Leno to my cell phone when I was walking on Madison Avenue. I stopped at a street corner to speak with the NBC show host, who expressed concern about some statements I had made in an interview that he perceived as being incorrect. It was the first and last time we spoke (cordially, and on a first-name basis), but the important point is that people in the public eye can break through the firewall of office privacy to get phone calls put through.

Status represents another overpriced subject that people want too much. Individuals will pay too much to preserve the image of rank and position. When I am up against a blue blood or a noted media or business personality in a divorce case, I know from experience that the need for status will play out to my advantage.

Over the years, I have represented women whose cases varied in details but had a common thread: These wives enjoyed a high standard of living, sometimes supported by the husband's earnings and sometimes by the husband's wealthy family. If the marriage had been a long one blessed with children, these wives stood an excellent chance of maintaining a high status and lifestyle. Problems arose in short-term marriages, particularly where a husband's family or the family inheritance had supported the high level of comfort. In these cases, the economic fall of the wife was abrupt and devastating. Often these wives cannot deal with the sudden loss of income, and their newfound reduction of wealth perpetuates cases that should never be continued.

In public cases, it is most often the wife who fears her former fame and status will slip away. During one divorce case, I remember looking through the diary of a woman who was married to a prominent man. I saw notes like; "Monday: Dinner with the Governor. Friday: Formal ball at the White House." In sadness, I had to reflect that this elegant lifestyle would be forever lost to her after the divorce. The famous husband still would be invited everywhere but she would fade into obscurity. Listen to the sad tales from divorced Hollywood wives whose exciting lives ended when their famous actor husbands filed for divorce.

COUNTRY CLUBS

Husbands frequently will pay an overvalued amount to remain a member of a country club. In a trade-off to the wife, they will pay a price that exceeds any utilitarian value of the membership.

Insistence on maintaining a connection in the country club reveals a man wanting too much. I often find husbands who do not play golf or tennis and may use the club only a few times a year. Yet in a divorce, they want to hang onto the membership. Perhaps husbands perceive that they can stay connected to a certain social class of men by continuing in the club.

In the past, country clubs often stipulated in the bylaws that divorced wives could not retain a membership in the country club but husbands could. The clause may have been financially based since husbands were then the main or sole income producers. Or the club may have foreseen possible ugly scenes if the ex-spouses remained comembers.

Today, many clubs do not insert these restrictive clauses. Instead they have categories like "primary" and "associate" memberships and permit divorced wives (usually, the associate) to stay in the club but only by elevating the membership to primary and paying the significant difference. Nevertheless, there will always be the potential for a nasty confrontation if one ex-spouse shows up at the club with a new, significant other while the other ex-spouse remains a member.

Couples who are wealthy as a result of a husband's income often start a charitable organization to save taxes. Under federal tax law, however, the charitable foundation must expend a certain amount of its income each year. Often, a divorced wife will not want to give up the option to pay for seats or tables at charity balls, which, in the past, were paid for by the family charity. In addition, these charitable donations are the coin that buys individuals places on boards of directors of hospitals or other charities. Serving on these boards confers a social status that the wife typically (but not always) seeks to continue. A wife may pay substantial money for the right to continue to use something that costs the husband nothing to give.

Not Taking Stock

Clients in divorce cases will ask whether they should keep shares of corporate stock in the settlement, hoping that the shares will increase over time. It is a fair question, but my recommendation is always to divest the stock received as part of the agreement.

During the dot-com craze, I represented a woman whose husband was a successful inventor in the technological sector.

He insisted on keeping the stock and the stock options in his publicly traded company, surrendering real estate and tangible cash assets to his wife for giving up the stock. A short time later, the technological bubble burst and his shares proved worthless. The husband had counted on the stock rising to great heights instead of treating the shares as one part of the settlement in the divorce. Greed had motivated the man; he wanted the stock too much and paid the price.

By the same token, where there has been a transfer of stock as a result of a divorce settlement, a wife sometimes will give me a bonus consisting of shares of the stock that she has acquired. By her computation, the gift of stock expresses appreciation and yet costs her nothing. In these cases, I always sell the stock at once. The law is my primary source of income, not the stock market.

In a divorce case, the wife's accountant and I received bonuses of stock from her portion of the settlement. I sold my shares but the accountant wavered, wondering whether to sell or keep his gift. He asked me several times for my advice, and I told him my rule was to sell the shares on receipt and never wait for the future. He sold his shares, and he still thanks me because a month later the company went out of business.

Avoiding Lawsuits

Some people have a pathological fear of lawsuits and will put clauses into contracts to prevent this kind of legal action. Their motivations are twofold: to avoid bad publicity and to keep control. A contract signed with a mandatory arbitration clause is an example of avoiding potential lawsuits.

The aversion to a possible lawsuit is akin to the unnecessary request for confidentiality. These "no lawsuit" clauses crop up in paternity cases or, more rarely, in breach of confidentiality clauses and in palimony cases. The person who insists on the clause will overpay for the privilege.

I have handled lots of paternity cases that follow the same script. At first, the man will deny the child is his while he waits for the HLA or DNA test results. As soon the test confirms paternity, we enter into the next stage of negotiation. As an aside, Sigmund Freud stated something like, "Maternity is always known while paternity is always inferred."

Men involved in paternity suits want the proceedings kept quiet. Fearing bad publicity from the press, they want to finish the case in a swift negotiation that rarely ends up in court. They also dread the possible divorce action from an outraged spouse, who is shocked to learn of hubby's extramarital dalliance and the arrival of his new little dividend. These variables force men to settle paternity suits in a hurry.

In July 1989, I represented Katherine Berkery in a paternity suit against the Las Vegas-based singing star, Tom Jones. At first, the Welsh born singer, one of the richest rockers from Britain (along with David Bowie and Paul McCartney), denied having a one-night fling in Manhattan with my client. He was vociferous in claiming that the child was not his and accused Ms. Berkery of being a gold digger. After meeting with her, my judgment was that she was anything but a gold digger. I found her a charming, soft-spoken woman who had succumbed to Mr. Jones's charms and now found herself with a child from that liaison.

At the time of the case, DNA expert Barry Scheck was known in very few legal circles and I was unfamiliar with his name. Years later, I met him in California during the O. J. Simpson trial, in which he performed brilliantly. I covered the O. J. case for the BBC and we compared notes. He reminded me that he had worked as the DNA legal expert in the Tom Jones paternity case when the tests indicated that the probability was 99.97 percent that Jones was the father of the child.

Back then with the forces of modern genetic biology stacked against him, Scheck was in a hopeless situation but he did as good a job as possible. He produced an expert on DNA, a professor from the Middle West, who testified that the child's father could have been any one of 80,000 white males. In cross-examination, I asked this DNA expert whether he believed any *one* of the 80,000 white males was present in Room 819 of the Essex House on April 15, 1989 (the date the child was conceived). Everyone in my court erupted in laughter, including the judge.

An unusual sidelight to this case was that it was the last one tried by Family Court Judge Sheindlin, who has now achieved fame and fortune as television's *Judge Judy*. In one of life's coincidences, she lives across the hall from me with her charming husband, who is a retired judge, and their poodle, also charming.

The Jones case was a no-holds-barred trial. At one point, Mr. Jones's lawyer accused my client of being the girlfriend of John Gotti. In those days, Gotti was not a man anyone wanted to annoy. The press carried the Gotti accusation, and soon the other lawyer telephoned to say he was apprehensive about his personal safety. The lawyer's worries existed more in his head than in reality because I am sure the Teflon Don could not have cared less. I hesitated to make this call, fearing that the conversation might put the idea of a "hit" in Gotti's head. The attorney made me promise to call up Gotti's personal attorney (which I did) and relay the message that the lawyer meant no disparagement by his offhand remark in cross-examination.

PATERNITY PAYMENTS

Most states have a provision allowing an accused father to make a deal for an up-front payment that is larger than the amount the court would award in terms of periodic payments. This provides the option of settling the case with a lump sum that can be invested to produce income for child support. In return for the one-time payout, the mother cedes any right to request additional funds as the years go by. It can be attractive to both parties: The mother can plan for the future based on the steady income stream she will receive over time, and the father does not have to worry about the mother coming back at him again and again in court for additional support.

Quickly settled paternity settlements go hand in hand with wealthy and public figures. After serving as Robin Givens's attorney, I represented a woman who had a child by Mike Tyson. He did not use the lump sum, one-time buyout provision but instead agreed to periodic payments that were subject to review every three years. Tyson seems to have bonded with this girl—I have seen her ringside at some of his fights. His public bankruptcy filing indicated that he was behind $60,000 in child support.

I also represented the mother of an out-of-wedlock child born to the son of boxing promoter, Don King (who managed Tyson). Years later, King was pleased to introduce me at an event as a lawyer who acts like a tiger that relentlessly stalks its prey. He is a humorous, intelligent man who sometimes refers to the Marion, Ohio, penitentiary where he was incarcerated as his "alma mater."

Prizefighters are a pleasure to represent. They are often gentle, noncombative, and reasonable. I represented former heavyweight champ Riddick Bowe and discovered that he was soft spoken and deferential. I saw a television replay of his three brutal bouts with Evander Holyfield, and I never would have believed that the polite person in my office was capable of such pugilistic aggression.

My office is across the street from the New York Palace Hotel. Late one afternoon, Bowe consulted with me for several hours. Since I had to see him again the next day, he offered to stay overnight in New York City instead of returning home to Maryland. He indicated a preference to stay at the swanky Palace Hotel.

I observed that he wore no sports jacket, had on a short-sleeve shirt and casual slacks, and carried no luggage, not even a briefcase. I assumed that the Palace Hotel would reject an under-dressed walk-in who did not even carry a toothbrush. I told Bowe that since I was going uptown, I would walk with him to the hotel. My hope was that since the hotel staff knew me on sight, they would register someone in my company.

As we approached the hotel, the people we met—from the front doorman, to the bellhops, to the room clerk inside—all said, "Hi, Riddick. How's it going champ?" The staff recognized him at first glance and extended warm cordiality. The Palace was de-lighted to have him as a guest and offered additional amenities. To this day, I am sure some of the staff wonders who that bearded fel-low in the suit was who walked in the hotel with Riddick Bowe.

I also represented Brazilian beauty, Luciana Morad, who had a child by rock star Mick Jagger. The DNA nailed the singer to the wall. Under legal arrangement, Jagger testified over speakerphone at his lawyer's office in London. The rest of the hearing was con-ducted in person in New York. When it came time for the money aspect of the proceeding, the other side hotly contested my right to financial information about Jagger's wealth and income since he was prepared to pay support. I succeeded in winning the right to have complete financial discovery, which was key to breaking the case, and Jagger soon settled for a large sum.

Having represented people in cases involving celebrities like Carson, Tom Jones, and Jagger over the years, I know that their finances, although legal in every sense, are structured to maxi-mize revenues and reduce the tax burden. International celebri-ties employ a battery of accountants and attorneys to minimize taxes by means of domicile or other tax requirements from the different jurisdictions in which they perform, live, or own homes.

In addition, few superstars (or any of the very rich) relish having people count their cash. It is even more damaging when a famous person's large income or estate is made public. In an ongoing attempt to embarrass New York Mayor Michael Bloomberg, his name never seems to be mentioned without reference to the $76 million he spent for the mayoral campaign.

Some performers also feel it does not help their careers if people who have paid half a week's salary for concert tickets are aware of the star's (e.g., Jagger's) mega-million-dollar income.

The Maltese Falcon

I admit that on one occasion I did not practice what I preach; I wanted an object too much. I coveted one of the seven original Maltese Falcon statues used in the 1941 Dashiell Hammett film classic directed by John Huston.

According to the history of the mythical statue, in 1539 the Knights Templar of Malta paid tribute to King Charles V of Spain by giving him a golden falcon encrusted from top to bottom with the rarest of jewels. Legend says that Barbary pirates seized the galley carrying the gift and stole the bejeweled statue. From that moment on, the Maltese Falcon vanished into myth and history.

For several years, I had been collecting film memorabilia, but my heart's desire was to acquire one of the Maltese Falcons. Christie's, the world-renowned auction house, announced that one of the statues would be coming on the auction market from the estate of the television actor, Robert Conrad. He had received it as a gift from Harry Warner (Warner Brothers had produced the film).

When the statue arrived in New York, Christie's invited me for a private showing. I held the heavy bird in my hand, and touching it increased my impassioned craving to add it to my collection. Few people know that six of the seven statues weighed a hefty 50 pounds each. One weighed less so that Humphrey Bogart could handle it on the movie set. And, yes, one of the seven statues contains the serrated scratch marks from Sydney Greenstreet's on-camera scraping.

The day of the auction, I calculated how high I was prepared to bid. A representative of the city of San Francisco (where the film's action took place) also attended but had a bidding cap of $25,000. The auction began and I sat in the room in a state of high anxiety. The spirited bids climbed higher and higher until I offered $300,000, which represented appreciably more than the highest amount I had *ever* been prepared to spend. Thank goodness, a person climbed to $400,000 for the winning bid. Imagine my returning home at night with the statue in hand and saying to my two children, "For $300,000 plus an extra $50,000 for sales tax and commission, look at the nice black bird Daddy purchased."

For years, I had speculated that if I ever acquired one of the statues, I would make a deal with a major jeweler to embed the statue with precious gems, as described in the movie. I would allow the jeweler to display it for a time, sell it, and then we would share in the profits. The falcon was purchased anonymously, or so I thought. Then the newspapers discovered the buyer was Harry Winston, the Fifth Avenue jewelry salon. What happened after that remains a mystery.

While I was bidding for the statue with avaricious acquisitiveness, somewhere in the back of my head I heard the precautionary words of Sol Goldman and I stopped further insanity. I left the auction house lucky that I had not spent a small fortune on a movie prop. I had to walk away from the object of my desire.

It was "The stuff that dreams are made of."

Sol Goldman

The name Sol Goldman appears several times in this book. Goldman was a master of the art of negotiation. He started with almost nothing, first owning an Italian-American grocery store in Brooklyn. He was able, through shrewd and intuitive bargaining, to amass a vast real estate fortune that in today's market would be worth billions of dollars.

Goldman achieved enormous wealth by adhering to his motto of never wanting anything so much that he could not walk away from it. I handled his drawn-out and fractious divorce, and during our conferences he told me interesting business and personal stories about his life. He was a negotiator supreme. After World War II until his death in 1987, Goldman and his partner, Alex DiLorenzo, were maverick real estate entrepreneurs. Unlike today's real estate barons, who employ public relations firms to enhance their reputations, the pair kept a sharp eye out for value while remaining indifferent to their own status or image.

The two Brooklyn-born partners never achieved the Manhattan real estate prestige of the Tishman brothers, Harry Helmsley, or Donald Trump. They never aspired to be among the city's real estate inner circle elite. Their reputation as rough-and-tumble, outer borough businesspeople worked in their favor as they purchased profitable buildings (residential walk-ups, warehouses, etc.) that other, more established firms would not touch. They ended up owning major real estate throughout New York City, including the Chrysler Building and a few famous hotels.

Over the years, Goldman and DiLorenzo expanded their thriving (and often) anonymous real estate operation. Goldman used the same sharp techniques on price to acquire prestigious sites as he used to negotiate leases with one-story houses in Brooklyn. One technique was to use aliases when inquiring about properties. He would instruct owners to call back and ask for "Mr. Fielding," a fabricated name at an office number that did not reveal the Goldman-DiLorenzo connection. DiLorenzo took the disguise one step further by using a fictitious name when he attended closings.

One time, Goldman was bidding for the office building at East Fourty-Second Street and Fifth Avenue and the price skyrocketed. Goldman shrugged his shoulders and said, "It's too rich for my blood" and walked away from the deal. He never had regrets about turning down a property.

Goldman was invited to meet the senior management of Chase-Manhattan Bank (the David Rockefeller institution) for the first time at the company's high-status headquarters on Wall Street. The invitation meant Chase recognized that Brooklyn billionaire Sol Goldman's business was worth pursuing. He arrived an hour late for the meeting, surprising the Chase executive staff with the reason for his tardiness: "I drove around and around and couldn't find a vacant parking space on the street so I had to park in a garage."

The garage story would have surprised no Goldman associate; he was always a down-to-earth guy. He never carried credit cards and always paid for everything in cash.

Goldman and his wife lived in a penthouse at the Stanhope Hotel on Fifth Avenue, a luxury Upper East Side property that he owned. But after he had to use his wooden cane to drive off a burglar in a second armed robbery, he felt compelled to move into a suite in the elegant Towers at the Waldorf-Astoria Hotel. The Towers are adjacent to the main hotel, with a separate entrance. Past, full-time residents have been Mrs. Douglas MacArthur and former President Herbert Hoover.

In 1986, Lillian, Sol Goldman's wife of 40 years, sued for divorce, an event that the New York press reported in great detail. I represented Sol and Lillian employed Roy Cohen and Arthur Lyman (noted for his legal work in the Iran-Contra Scandal). In court, she claimed, among other accusations, that Sol had tried to hurl her out a window at the Waldorf Towers. A statement like this is so inflammatory that an attorney has to squelch it right away—an entire judgment can hang on the scorching accusation.

I had to put this scandalous fire out without delay. Another couple, who now lived in the same suite that the Goldmans had previously occupied in the Towers, allowed us to enter the suite. We did so accompanied by representatives of the Waldorf who watched our every action as though we were going to steal the furniture or filch an ashtray. I also brought along a photographer, an architect, and an engineer. We went to all the windows in the suite and tried to open them. None of us, alone or working together, could budge open any window.

When Sol lived in this room, he walked with a cane, suffered from kidney problems, and was on dialysis three times a week. It was not feasible that he could have lifted his hefty wife, thrown her over the ledge covering the windows' radiators, and hurled her through windows that no one could open. The final proof came from the Waldorf, which kept impeccable historical records. Rechecking its files, the hotel found out that the windows had been sealed in 1936.

In New York, then as now (as in some other states), a wife cannot obtain equitable distribution of the marital assets unless she can prove she is entitled to a divorce. Sol took the position that he loved his wife and did not want to end the marriage. Lillian had no case when faced with the realization that her causes of action for divorce were false and would not stand up in court. On the eve of trial, she settled the dispute after consultation with her lawyers. In the settlement, she would receive a huge portion of the estate when Sol died, but there would be no division of assets during his life.

We anticipated that the Goldmans would reconcile so that, while Sol lived, he would continue to pay Lillian's regular living expenses. But her living costs exceeded what anyone else would consider normal. She steamed because the reconciliation notwithstanding, she had been thwarted in her efforts to obtain huge sums of money in the divorce action. Returned to her wifely status, she would remain under her husband's financial thumb.

Months later, I received a letter from Roy Cohen. He complained that Sol Goldman, unbeknownst to me, had not yet paid his legal bill. It is often customary for husbands to pay the legal fees of the wife's attorney. Cohen wrote, "My bill is long overdue. Please, remind Sol of what we did for him." The "we did" referred to the fact that Cohen and I helped in the couple's attempt at reconciliation. The meaning was clear to me, and I had the letter hand-delivered to Sol. Later, I discussed the letter from Cohen, believing Sol would either pay or negotiate the attorney's fee with Cohen one on one.

As a result of Cohen's innocent letter, the delicate Goldman marital situation exploded one night, months after they had reconciled. That evening Lillian rummaged through Sol's pants pockets and discovered the Cohen note. She spotted the part that read "what we did for him" and flew into rage, assuming erroneously that she had been betrayed. She tried to prove that Sol, Roy Cohen, and I colluded against her interests in the first divorce action. She mounted a publicized lawsuit, alleging fraud and moved to set aside the original reconciliation agreement.

The *New York Times* carried Lillian's accusation that Cohen and I had collaborated and forced her to agree to the separation agreement. There was no truth to the accusation; she was trying to shake Sol down for more money. A quick or a nonsophisticated reading of the short article, however, would indicate that the events described had occurred. I called the *New York Times* and complained that Lillian had lied; it was not even a question of stretching the truth. The editor said the paper would not retract the article but assured me that if I was victorious, the paper would run a story of equal size. I was vindicated when the judge found no evidence to support her reckless charges. No one ever saw this correction in the newspaper—if it was ever written.

Sol was healthy aside from his kidney problem. It might be years before Lillian would receive the vast sums from his estate under the agreement that she now sought to set aside with a new team of attorneys. She wanted to get control of the monies as soon as possible and not wait for her husband's death. The case wound its way through the New York court system until it came up for trial.

I considered it to be a piece of bad luck when I learned that the trial judge would be Kristen Booth Glen. I had no particular ill feelings against this judge, but she appeared to hate me, an opinion that also seemed evident to my staff. My own observation was that she was an intelligent person with all kinds of emotional and psychological crosscurrents and complications. She was a zealous feminist with a chip on her shoulder, who saw men as a threat to her power. The gender issue dangled like the proverbial Sword of Damocles in her courtroom and often represented a needless hindrance to male attorneys.

I was always tempted to say in my closing statement, "Your Honor, let me remind the court that my wife is a *female* practicing attorney whom I encouraged to go to law school, and I paid in full this *female's* tuition." Judge Glen treasured those lawyers who practiced in the Grovel School of Jurisprudence. I never studied at this school.

The Goldman case became attenuated, it stretched on with Judge Glen taking several months to make a decision. In 1987, when Sol was almost at his deathbed, the judge ruled, "There was not a scintilla of evidence that supported the plaintiff's [Mrs. Goldman] version of events." If we search carefully, we usually can discover collateral bits of confirmation to support one person's or another's perception of past events. This case was no exception. We relied on telephone records and other independent evidence to substantiate our version of what had happened when Sol, Roy Cohen, and I were together.

While the battling Goldmans were locked in acrimonious litigation, Lillian was diagnosed as having cancer and needed an immediate operation. When Sol heard this news, he grew concerned and gave instructions to me to make sure their children found the best surgeons for her treatment and the best hospital care. He asked that all medical bills be sent to him for payment, with but one stipulation, "Don't tell Lillian."

I have witnessed similar acts of care and kindness when long-standing marriages break up. The ties that bind and the feelings built up over a long marriage are more meaningful than the hot debate or acrimony in the courtroom. I often see a husband become irate when someone (his own lawyer, the judge, or whoever) speaks in a rude tone to his wife in court, even though the couple is in the midst of hard-fought adversarial litigation. I have tried to understand this on a human level and have asked husbands why they show this tender behavior in divorce proceedings. Almost always, I receive a variation of one of the following two responses: "She is the mother of my children, and I do not want her spoken to in this rude manner"; or "I do not hate my wife; I just want to give her as little money as possible."

In 1987, Sol Goldman died. At this point, Lillian's embarrassing court defeat turned into victory. After his death, she received the money as the main beneficiary of his estate, as stipulated in the agreement. She spent it in lavish ways, few of which would have been her husband's choice. She endowed the Lillian Goldman Law Library at Yale University Law School, which was incongruous because Sol Goldman did not like lawyers (especially, "fancy" lawyers) and would not have wanted to support a law school located in New Haven, Connecticut. He would have preferred a tribute in New York City, the city he loved; and he did achieve a wonderful memorial with the new Sol Goldman YM-YWHA on East 14th Street in Manhattan.

This story has some interesting postscripts, most of them bad. Roy Cohen died of AIDS, discredited, broke, and disbarred. Kristin Booth Glen left the bench to become Dean of CUNY Law School, and—to be charitable—has done a mediocre job. The law school has continued to place very low in a U.S. law school poll conducted by *U.S. News and World Report.* One reason for the poor ranking is the low number of the school's graduates who pass the bar. One of her pet projects at CUNY was building a leafy garden labyrinth at the law school. She said, "It just seems to me that we have an obligation to give our students and graduates some tools to deal with stress." Under her aegis came weekly yoga and meditation classes as well as the labyrinth as part of a stress reduction contemplative program. Justice Learned Hand is not resting peacefully in his grave.

A final addendum to the Sol Goldman never-want-too-much story: I brought to his attention the long property list of items he and Lillian had acquired during their marriage. Lillian was a shopaholic, who also liked to bargain.

Sol laughed, "Lillian was a terrific negotiator but she *never* could walk away from anything."

ESTABLISHING
CREDIBILITY

Even with the new no-fault divorce system, clients still want to hire a lawyer to be an instrument of revenge. Some clients have less interest in obtaining the most money from a settlement than in destroying the other party in a final and rancorous battle to the end. But my goal is never to settle personal scores; it is always to make the best settlement.

In a court, an omnibus reason attorneys give to the judge to allow material evidence during cross-examination is, "It goes to credibility." In a larger sense, everything about a person goes to his or her credibility. In negotiations, having credibility is imperative; its loss is a serious matter.

When I moved into a new neighborhood in Manhattan, I visited a local, popular seafood store on First Avenue. It catered to retail purchasers and supplied some of the better restaurants in the city. The second time I visited the store, I noticed that it sold prepared soups. I took a jar of clam chowder out of the refrigerator cabinet and was about to pay for it when the fishmonger said, "Sir, don't take the chowder, it's not from today." The man established instant credibility, and to this day I have accepted his recommendations and have never purchased a bad or stale piece of fish.

APPEARANCE

A person's appearance contributes to that individual's credibility. If life is a series of ongoing steps to sell oneself in matters of love or work, appearance represents an important component of the sale. Oscar Wilde summed this up in *The Picture of Dorian Gray*: "It is only shallow people who do not judge by appearances. The true mystery of the world is the visible, not the invisible."

Clothes may or may not make the man but the right attire can help establish credibility. As costumes, clothes allow us to play different parts based on the history of people who once dressed in those clothes. Lawyers engaged in the practice of criminal law are cognizant of how clients will be perceived, and that is why a defendant never appears in court looking unshaved or wearing old clothes.

In the murder trial of the infamous Menendez brothers, their two lawyers dressed the matricide and patricide shotgun killers in crew-neck sweaters and chinos to make them resemble innocent boys. The "barefoot boys with cheek of tan" look helped in portraying the brothers, not as mature men in their twenties capable of slaughtering their parents, but as blameless teenagers who were the true victims in a bad family.

Leslie Abramson, Erik Menendez's attorney, created a melodramatic play entitled, *The Troubled Aunt and the Victimized Nephew*, in which she acted out an in-court relationship. During the trial, she picked lint off her client's sweater and engaged in other personal and intimate actions. Her behavior effectively told the jury that she, as a credible attorney, was not defending a heinous monster, but a misunderstood boy who had been mistreated by fiendish parents.

In the first trial, this earnest-young-boys-in-school appearance helped set the stage for two hung juries. The women in the two juries would not budge to vote for more serious charges than manslaughter. In the second trial, the brothers were dressed in shirts and ties and looked like men in their twenties, not teenagers. It was easier for the prosecution to "go for credibility" and describe the brothers as ruthless killers when the first trial's juvenile image did not reappear in court.

Everyone knows the importance of dressing for court. In fact, I tell my female clients to wear a simple black outfit and pearls. If they have wild or flowing tresses, I tell them either to get their hair trimmed or roll it into a neat bun.

Early in my career, I represented my brother's former songwriting partner, Mort Shuman in a divorce case. Shuman was well known for writing the hit off-Broadway show *Jacques Brel Is Alive and Well in Paris.* He had a flamboyant personality, dressing with a flare for clothes as befits a wealthy dandy with piles of money. I told him he had to forgo the foppery and come to court dressed humbly. I instructed him to wear the same suit each day so that the jury would build up a positive identification enhanced by simple clothes.

When he told me he did not own any humble suits, I accompanied him to Howard Clothes, a chain of stores that specialized in $19 suits. He bought a cheap one off the rack and wore it to court each day; at the end of the trial, we participated in a ceremonial burning of the "humble" suit.

Often, when jailhouse stool pigeons testify in criminal cases, prosecutors will try to dress them in mufti instead of letting them appear in the orange uniforms issued by many states. Establishing credibility for convicts as trustworthy witnesses is more difficult if the jurors view them in the prison garb, which is a reminder that they have committed felony crimes.

Few people today remember Carmine De Sapio, the last old-time Tammany Hall boss in New York City. He had succeeded in electing Robert Wagner mayor of New York City in 1953 and Averill Harriman as governor of New York in 1954. His downfall stemmed from a reform movement led by Eleanor Roosevelt to form the New York Committee for Democratic Voters, which removed the political boss from power in 1961.

De Sapio was front-page news for the city's tabloids, and his photographs were easy to recognize because he wore large sunglasses. The public was left with the impression that De Sapio was a shady character who hid truth behind the dark glasses. The reality was that De Sapio suffered from an eye condition and had to wear the dark shades to block out light. When he was on trial for criminal charges, he wore the dark glasses to court. The legal consensus was that his glasses contributed to the guilty verdict. I am reminded of the last line in the first *King Kong* film, "It wasn't planes; 'twas beauty that killed the beast." The sunglasses "killed" Carmine De Sapio's credibility.

CREDIBILITY FOR WIVES

In divorce cases, stay-at-home wives do not have the same credibility as their more famous husbands. Society rates housewives, in particular women without independent careers, as second-class citizens compared with their successful captains-of-industry husbands. These men, who often have important commercial positions, assume that their power filters into the legal system to make them a *primus inter pares*, a first among equals.

In one divorce case, I represented the wife, a successful physician who married a workaholic business executive from Long Island. For years, he had been the number two executive at a small company that was very family oriented. It seemed to him that as a lifelong bachelor he could attain the top office by marrying. He assured my client that after the nuptials, his obsessive work habits would change. These were hollow words, and months after the wedding when he assumed the president's position, he reverted to putting in 18-hour workdays and working at the office on weekends.

A year later, the wife sued for divorce. Since she had a high income and owned a New York apartment, the divorce seemed straightforward. She asked for nothing. But a recurrent problem arose each time we went to court; the husband never appeared. Over a period of months, the judge, whom I knew to be fair and pragmatic, grew more and more impatient with the no-show husband. He directed the opposing counsel to bring the husband in for conference dates to discuss a speedy and uncomplicated dissolution of the marriage. My adversary was unable to overcome the executive's arrogance and could not persuade him to make an appearance.

The judge issued a final warning; either the husband would show or the judge would rule without him and also consider issuing a contempt citation. The day arrived, and at the stipulated time, the man was absent. The judge granted the divorce and also ordered the husband cited for contempt of court and ordered him to pay a large fine. As we left the courthouse parking lot, the husband arrived albeit too late. We heard him shout a loud expletive when his lawyer told him the judge's decision.

LOSING CREDIBILITY

A recurrent problem in my divorce cases is that wives fail to heed my admonition not to discuss our conversations with their spouses. I have established credibility with the husbands and their attorneys, and this is diminished when wives blurt out statements, frequently in anger, about our strategy. A wife can destroy a day's hard work with a loose tongue. Time and again in representing a wife, we have gone one step forward during the day, and then she has taken two steps backward during the night, making it difficult to proceed with the case.

Husbands assume that their wives have become nonpeople or persons without rights. But when women hire lawyers, they attain instant credibility. Arrogant men accustomed to giving business underlings orders, meet their match when the wives make demands for child support, disclosure of assets, business records, and other motions that require the husband's personal attendance in court. The husband soon realizes that the judge is calling the shots.

It is a rule of practice in legal proceedings not to substitute a lawyer's credibility for a client's. The reason for the rule prohibiting the lawyer as witness is that the rectitude of attorneys should not stand in place of the client's. Of course, since lawyers encounter the same group of adversaries, the same cast of characters time after time, we are the worst offenders when it comes to credibility.

DAVID SUSSKIND

In 1986, I represented Joyce Davidson Susskind in a divorce against her then famous husband David Susskind, one of television's most prolific producers and the father of the talk show format. He conversed with thousands of guests on a wide range of topics, including abortion, civil rights, and drugs. And he moderated these talks in his own style, which could be described as informative, combative, and blunt. Whether viewers concurred or disagreed with his opinions, they regarded him as knowledgeable and credible.

When I met Susskind, he appeared unimpressive. Sure, he sounded great, but what he said was banal. At the courthouse, standing in the hall between proceedings, he started to talk to me. I turned away for an instant, smiling at a remark somebody else next to me had made. In that moment, Susskind lost control and said, "I'm going to knock the smile off your face." The threat sounded even more ridiculous because Susskind was a much older man. I could see he was trembling with anger, and I walked away, leaving him impotently frothing. Then I had a real smile on my face.

THE NAME GAME

In a negotiation, remembering someone by his or her first name establishes a positive connection and creates a "cordiality baseline." Most politicians have acquired the skill of remembering first names, and even when they do not, they cover it up well. When you can recall names, it helps your creditability.

Former New York City mayor David Dinkins would call me "counselor," but it was clear he did not remember my first name. Former Vice-President Nelson Rockefeller would greet me with, "Hi, ya, fella." But many other political figures have mastered this skill of recalling first names. Former New York City mayors Rudy Giuliani, and the late Robert Wagner come to mind, as do Presidents George W. H. Bush and George W Bush.

Some entertainers are also memory experts. I have represented Bobby Short the extraordinary cafe society entertainer for 40 years. I am continually amazed how he remembers the first names of his countless thousands of fans.

I have never been able to master the art of remembering names. Sherlock Holmes noted that the brain is like an attic—once it gets filled up there is no room for anything else. While I can remember the facts of a case for many years, I often draw a blank on people's names. Neurologists that I have consulted say that this is not a function of an aging mind but, as we grow older, a sophisticated selection process takes place. Facts are important. They stay in the attic. Names are less important.

FINAL WORDS

Advertising agencies often use distinguished-looking people or celebrities to give instant credibility to a product. Think of those bygone commercials where a man in a doctor's white jacket would tout an over-the-counter medication. The uniform bespoke physician, and physician connoted credibility.

One of my favorite ads featured a man who said, "I am not a real doctor, I only play one on television" and then went on to talk about the product. Credibility emerges from establishing the bona fides. It stems from age and experience and also from delivering on promises.

My friend Howard Koeppel maintains the credibility of his VW franchise by using savvy negotiation skills. Here's what he says:

> My first rule of negotiation, whether it's for an automobile or some other type of contract, is always to start high because then you can always lower the price down. But if you start low, you can never go up.
>
> Negotiation is letting the customer know that he's gotten a terrific deal but also negotiating the best deal for myself. I call this happy medium the comfort level and it's where both parties are satisfied.
>
> If I let a customer walk out with a car where I have made too large a profit, I can replace the car but not the customer. Conversely, in some inventory situations, I may have one car too many and can let it go for a lower amount. My comfort level is lower but I've probably made a customer for life.

Credibility is making and keeping a friend or a customer for life.

WALKING OUT

In the 1930 motion picture *Animal Crackers*, Groucho Marx played Captain Spaulding and sang this refrain, "Hello I must be going. I cannot stay; I came to say I must be going. I am glad I came, but just the same, I must be going."

When negotiations get tough and nasty, the savvy negotiator often gets going because walking out is an effective tactic. It is the most effective and unequivocal way to say "enough" and to emphasize that any amicable dialogue is over. Leaving can be the doomsday card that you play when the discussions have reached a standstill and you realize that further debate will not produce progress. Because no one can continue to make conversation with an empty chair, walking out becomes the last word. In effect, sometimes the optimum exit strategy is *the* exit strategy.

Make the walkout a stylized performance and punctuate it in high dramatic style. The moment when you rise from your seat to leave should resemble the conclusion of a spirited musical performance, much like the resounding end to a can-can at the Moulin Rouge or the cannons going off at the end of the *1812* Overture. The music accelerates faster and faster until a crescendo swells to the top and then pauses before the distinct, earsplitting clang of the cymbals. Then you are gone in an over-the-top flourish, showing your back to the room.

The goal is to close the door on the negotiations but the last words you say will leave open an opportunity for future talks based on those words. This final speech before the exit is critical since it conveys the reasons for the sudden exit. If I say, "It's too expensive a deal" or "You leave us no room for compromise," then I have explained my sudden departure. My adversaries will remember the parting statement and not brood over why I exited the room and will understand the reasons holding up the resolution.

Union negotiations constitute the prime example of both the impending threat and the actuality of walking out. The wringing of hands after rejection of the last offer signals that the union delegation will be leaving the meeting for good. After the walkout is the strike, which is the last card in the first round of negotiations.

My father used the dramatic exit in his legal career most often with neighborhood clients who did not want to pay their bills. The implied threat was always the same. At the door, he would shout, "Okay, don't pay me. You don't owe me anything." These clients were afraid the neighbors would believe that they were cheapskates or that they would try to rip somebody else off. The dispute was not over whether they owed money, but "How much?" No one in our close-knit Brooklyn neighborhood—where everyone knew everyone else's business—wanted to be called a welsher. The clients always paid, but it required a theatrical departure with histrionic flamboyance to clinch the deal.

The walkout has to be done in cold blood—not hot blood. Do not be vituperative or make negative personal statements. The action is similar to the quick hit by the point of a fencer's épée; a single light thrust that stings on the touch. You do not want to bring out a heavy saber and slash off the enemy's head, leaving a bloodied torso.

DEALING WITH ULTIMATUMS

I had to walk out of a settlement conference because my adversary gave me no choice. She gave me an ultimatum. The meeting took about five minutes from the opening remark to my storming out.

The lawyer on the other side had called the meeting, which I anticipated would include the usual rehearsed opening remarks concerning the details of the case. When I inquired about the topic of the talks, she demanded the maximum monetary exposure for my client. Further, she presented it as an inflexible sum that my client would have to pay to settle the case. I delivered a firm message, saying, "What is the point of this meeting? You are not serious?" Then I walked out. The lawyer could not believe I exited. My action taught her a lesson for the next time we met—I would not accept a "my way or the highway" challenge. She would not want to deal the same way again with an opponent who ridiculed her demands by an abrupt departure.

It makes more sense to give people an escape route, a way to leave the field of battle with dignity or at least some methodology for saving face in a settlement. When the only path open to an adversary leads to destruction, you will witness the start of a long and terrible battle. The strategy would work fine if victory could be certain, but in negotiation no one can guarantee a favorable outcome.

WHEN THEY WALK OUT

There have been a few times when adversaries have walked out on me. Either they were fearful of losing, or they were unprepared and anticipated that they could play me for more time. My opponents have but one chance to pull this stunt because if I recognize the ploy as repetition in their bag of tricks, I refuse to negotiate with them in the future.

A small group of lawyers in New York City walk out at the least provocation. Some have reputations for staging exits to impress a client with a macho, take-no-prisoners stance. These attorneys want to create a scene to display that they are the cock of the walk. They will flagellate themselves into such a rancorous stew that the anger lifts them up and out of the room. If this occurs, I make the right play and never plead with them to stay. I never rush to bring them back to the bargaining table because then they will have gained the upper hand. The person left behind by the walkout is at a disadvantage because the dynamic in the room has switched.

Sometimes, after opposing lawyers have stormed out of my conference room, I find them in another room in my office making telephone calls or going over case points with their clients. I ask myself: How serious was the walkout if they are still here? I interpret their halfway exit to represent a subtle desire to return to the table.

When walking out, head straight to the elevator or the outer hall. The departure from the field of battle will have impact only if you disappear. If you stage a halfway exit one time, your opponents will not believe you are serious when you storm out on another occasion. Credibility dictates leaving the premises for good.

When people walk out in anger, they often leave papers behind on the conference table. If that happens, I make it a point to tell a secretary to put the papers in an envelope unread and send it to the lawyer. Other lawyers have told me that, to their regret, they left behind important documents that were embarrassing or should have been withheld from an adversary. The moral: Make sure the table is clean before exiting.

Exit Timing

The best time to bolt is when you are deep into the deliberations. After the negotiations have proceeded for weeks or months, the walkout has meaning, sending a strong communication that the deliberations cannot go any further and that you are giving up.

You must time the walkout perfectly: Neither make the exit too soon in the process nor stay too long in the negotiations. If you overstay the time at the table, you will be caught in a forever situation and a walkout will have little effect. The curtain has to be pulled down at a reasonable conclusion of the act. This consolidates what already has been agreed on, and allows the next session for unresolved matters.

There are times when a walkout is not a walkout. It is a mechanism to disrupt the adversary's timing. One of my tricks is to prearrange a departure. My secretary will come into the conference room at a prescheduled time to announce, "Mayor Bloomberg is on the phone." My adversaries are left standing with nothing to do. I have left, but it does not seem like a walkout. Instead, I have broken up their rhythm. It will be difficult for my opponents to return to form, and when they do, it will be from a stationary start. It will take time for them to build up to full speed again.

Bad Walkouts

Some walkouts have proved disastrous; especially among unions that overestimated their importance and self-worth to the community. Unions need to walk a delicate tightrope, balancing the demands and the threat of the walkout with the possibility that another strike might sound a death knell to the union.

At one time, almost all residential and office buildings in New York City had an elevator operator to take passengers from one floor to another. The operators' union wielded enormous power because of the operators' essential, 24-hour responsibility. But improvements in technology together with the union's wage demands and featherbedding arrogance soon changed the dynamic. Building owners grew tired of being held hostage to the constant and escalating requests of the union. Their solution was to convert to automatic elevators although it represented a substantial capital outlay. Forty years ago, at an average conversion cost of about $40,000 per elevator, it took an outlay of over $300,000 to convert an office building with a bank of eight elevators. Even so, owners of most of the older buildings, as well as any new ones under construction, opted for the automatic elevators as a one-time cost that they could amortize over time. More important, an automatic system had no need of a daily staff of round-the-clock operators.

The union reacted to the conversions by staging a series of walkouts to convince management of the crucial need for operators. The sudden walkouts emphasized the greedy union's recurring demands. One by one, buildings in New York changed to the automatic system, which proved safe and reliable and functioned without any employee wage or pension costs. In Rockefeller Center, one elevator operator is still employed to take the few nervous passengers up to the Rainbow Room.

The newspaper unions' battle with the publisher of the *New York Herald Tribune* is another historic example of a self-destructive walkout. The wealthy John "Jock" Hay Whitney had served as ambassador to Great Britain from 1957 to 1961; in 1958, his company acquired control of the *Herald Tribune;* and in 1961 he became its publisher.

The paper was losing money, and Whitney hoped that the various newspaper guilds, particularly the printer's union, would lower their demands. During negotiations, however, the union pressed for higher wages and fewer hours. Whitney threw up his hands and stated, "I am closing the newspaper." The head of the printer's union scoffed at the possibility, threatening to go to court to prevent the *Herald Tribune* from closing. The unions staged a walkout, and Whitney shut the paper down forever. The courts had no jurisdiction to stipulate that management must keep open a money-losing business.

When I had established a private practice and enjoyed some financial success, my support personnel and staff lawyers came to me en masse demanding across-the-board raises. Since I was faced with a solid phalanx, I asked them, "What alternative do I have?" The answer was that I had none. I pressed them further and asked what they would do if I did not give in to their demands. They replied they would leave, believing that they had placed me in an impossible situation. I next asked, "When?" but did not receive an answer. I then said, "How about tomorrow morning?" and I fired the ungrateful pack. In *The Maltese Falcon*, when Sam Spade gave over Brigid O'Shaughnessy to the police, he observed that he would have some "rough days." I had some rough days, but I survived (better than my former employees did), and the event came to be known in my office as the "Thursday Night Massacre."

One reason taxicab owners do not go on strike more often is the empirical knowledge that people who are forced to ride subways and buses will become accustomed to using them. In the past when taxi strikes were settled, a lot of former taxi riders stayed with public transportation.

MR. MERRICK

Broadway superproducer David Merrick was shrewd, successful, and reputedly not a very nice person. He possessed a fine creative sense but lacked the even-tempered capacity to negotiate with theatrical unions. He believed that since his money provided jobs to everyone onstage and backstage, they should react with gratitude. The craft unions (carpenters, electricians, lighting designers, etc.) failed to share Merrick's mind-set.

During one union negotiation with the International Alliance of Theatrical Stage Employees (IATSE), Merrick's combative stance and constant issuing of ultimatums drove the union representatives out of the room. At the time, he had several shows running on Broadway, and a walkout would have crippled the business. A theater that is dark generates no revenues.

Merrick realized that he had to resume negotiations or his productions would be in serious financial trouble. But he knew that he had so alienated the opposition in the first round of talks that even the sight of him returning to the bargaining table would open old wounds. He was smart enough to sense that his overbearing, bossy persona and plantation mentality would continue to enrage the union negotiators.

Faced with this dilemma, Merrick took the only step open to him: He asked an associate to take over and to deal with the unions. After a walkout, the key to resumption of negotiations is to use a third party to handle future talks. Merrick chose Mort Mitofsky, a lawyer and a theatrical agent, as well as a trusted friend. Mitofsky was well known to the union and did not carry the same negative baggage as the spoiling-for-a-fight Merrick.

Merrick's inherent distrust of employees is well documented. He believed that the people who worked in the ticket office were charging customers higher prices than the face value of the tickets and pocketing the difference. Merrick went to one of the box offices to investigate, hiking his coat collar up around his face and pulling a hat over his eyes to pretend he was an anonymous customer. At the ticket window, he said he wanted two tickets for *Subways Are for Sleeping*, and hinted he would pay *any price*. The ticket seller said, "Mr. Merrick, why are you buying tickets? You can have tickets for free." Merrick stormed away.

Exiting for All Occasions

In heated negotiations, there are times to stay and times to depart. For the latter, it will be those moments when someone brings up a topic that has no relevance or seems like a surprise issue designed to torpedo talks. Or it might be an ultimatum that signals the dead end to further deliberations.

Play a walkout as you would a violin. Another simile is that it is like a first kiss, you must time it judiciously and with some panache. When staging your exit, go all the way out the door because pausing or hesitation will lessen the impact and might even reduce your sudden departure to nothing.

Do not use the walkout step too often. If you develop a reputation as a chronic bolter, adversaries will perceive the walkout as a familiar and meaningless ploy and will disregard it. The same is true for threatening to walk out without ever doing so because then you will be remembered as the boy who cried wolf. Opponents know that you will return to the room after some halfhearted beseeching.

Walking out can be a risky move, putting an end to talks. It should be the last card you play when all the prior attempts have failed. As the final word, it delivers a powerful message that something is amiss in the deliberations. Walkouts are a dramatic substitute for Western Union. Use them sparingly, but execute them with élan and spirit.

 6

OPPONENTS

Negotiations are warfare, culminating with a triumphant victor and a defeated foe. I repeat: It is never wise to annihilate an opponent because you may have to deal with that adversary in the future. This is true not only in business but also in the day-to-day social negotiations between family and friends. If I go toe to toe with an opposing lawyer and the discussions grow heated or even hostile, we both may walk away with ruffled feathers at the end of the meeting, but we walk away. If I cannot control my anger and go for the jugular with my wife, children, staff, or close business associates, I may make that winning point but pay a costly financial and lasting emotional price.

Divorce is an excellent occasion to practice the art of winning with grace. A person can negotiate a wonderful settlement but the fact remains that a former spouse will continue in the person's life if they have children. Too often, I have witnessed gratuitous gloating by one party with the subsequent sad result that the "loser" poisons the minds of the children in a retaliatory act of blind revenge. My advice is to achieve a delicate balance to obtain victory, but not victory at all costs. The goal is to win and to allow the other side to withdraw with dignity.

I advise new lawyers that they should leave an opponent a small window to save face. If lawyers give ultimatums, even if they win, they will lose in the long effort. The other side should be able to claim victory in some area of the dispute.

If I win a preliminary point in court, instead of allowing my client to exult in the triumph, I caution against an overt cackle of boastful crowing. I want my client to realize that the other side cannot make an overture to resolve the case because it will approach in weakness and be burdened by defeat. When I win an interim legal step, I make it a practice to reach out to the opposition and say, "Isn't this a terrible waste of time and energy? Why not sit down and negotiate?"

Michael Hess, former Corporation Counsel (or chief lawyer) for New York City, and now a partner in the firm of Giuliani Partners, offers these helpful hints about opponents:

> If your goal is to destroy an opponent, it will be a losing strategy because victory will be gained at a high price when meeting this person again. What might occur the next time is that you may lose and your adversary will remember the salt poured on his wound. Whenever I know I am victorious, I try to be as conciliatory as possible and go for a quick and fair settlement.

In the movie *Havana*, Robert Redford played a professional gambler. He explained why he liked to play poker against politicians, whom he regarded as easy marks. He said that savvy gamblers would often lose at the beginning, even folding a winning hand, so later they could win with a losing hand. Politicians, he explained, never understood the gambler's strategy. They would leap on paltry victories, expending that stake, only to lose later in a much larger stake.

WINNING THE FIRST ROUND

One reason I win most preliminary points is that I make it a practice to do battle on winnable issues. This is an important tip: If possible, choose the battlefield that is slightly tilted in your favor. None of us can win a tennis point off Andrew Agassi or score a basket against Michael Jordan. The trick to winning is to play chess against Agassi and cribbage against Jordan.

My counsel is not to fight the smaller items unless these are easily winnable. Small interim victories do not mean ultimate victory, but small interim defeats can mean ultimate failure. Quoting Churchill again, whose words at the end of World War I rang prophetically true about the tragic future of Europe, "Victory was bought so dear as to be almost indistinguishable from defeat."

In labor negotiations, key elements are the number of days to be worked per week, vacation days, or days of sick time. A minor collateral issue may be that the workers in the union must start work on time because it is anticipated that work starts at 9 A.M. and stops at 5 P.M. If I were representing management, I would do battle on the issue that work must begin at 9 o'clock sharp. Labor unions employ a scorched-earth policy and will fight for every bit of ground. Their negotiators will argue for a 9:15 A.M. start time to be combative from the get-go. Making this 9 A.M. starting time the first line of battle assures a certain winner for my side, and it will place me in a better position to negotiate other points. I have won the first round.

TIMING

It is a propitious to know the time to commence negotiations. Delay often works against you. Imagine that a husband catches a wife in an act of adultery. This becomes a pendulum situation when she visits a divorce lawyer. At one end of the pendulum, she feels contrite and guilt-ridden, and may agree to any of the husband's demands. Now the pendulum begins to swing toward the middle with the wife saying, "What I did was a terrible betrayal, but horrible as my actions were, I still have rights." Now the pendulum moves beyond the midpoint, and she states, "My rights are my rights, which were solidified before I committed adultery, not after it." Then the pendulum swings full to the other side. She comments, "He was a lowlife who's been cheating on me with other women for years. Look what a hypocrite he is. I want to go after him full throttle."

It is said that in war no negotiation occurs until after the final battle. The end of hostilities signals the beginning of peace talks. However, what is applicable for war is not good strategy for day-to-day discussions. While life goes on after negotiated settlements, I advise young lawyers never to save the fancy steps for the Saturday night dance. Saturday night may never come. In other words, fire all the weapons in a particular negotiation and do not consider that you *might* want to use them later in the dispute.

On occasion, a client will say, "I do not want to introduce that evidence [or knowledge or document]. I will use it later on if we encounter trouble." That is not good strategy because you need to hit with maximum force when you go to battle. The secret of negotiation success is to use your weapons early on, not to wait until the battle's outcome.

The goal with an opponent is to have a give-and-take that is spirited but also flexible and reasonable. The polarizing observations of Otto von Bismarck sum up the disparity of how to deal with an adversary. At one end of the spectrum is to act aggressively with "iron and blood," and at the other end is a more pacific approach where "Politics [negotiation] is the art of the possible." Having said this, an unreal reality continues about negotiations in life itself.

It sounds cruel and heartless but the best time to hit opponents is when they are down. Assume it is a husband-and-wife negotiation, and I represent the wife. The husband may be upset because he lost an important client the week before. Putting aside the economic ramifications, nothing is wrong with my bringing matters to a head while he is gloomy. I am taking a situational advantage, proper in love, war, and negotiations.

One line I never cross. If a person is ill in the hospital or a loved one is dying, I do not serve papers or start negotiations. But there are people (even lawyers) who are guilty of the most offensive kinds of conduct in this regard.

A lawyer was in the midst of his own divorce case and another lawyer represented him. In PAGE SIX, the gossip column of the *New York Post*, it was reported that while the case was gong on, the divorcing lawyer's wife committed suicide. In a coffee shop near the court, the two lawyers were overhead gloating over her death. It was ugly, offensive, and in the worst possible taste.

DIVIDE AND CONQUER

I try to create a subtle but ethical flying wedge between opposing attorneys and their clients. On rare occasions, I may be able to tip the scales of a judge's decision my way by driving a wedge between the judge and the other lawyer.

At settlement meetings, I often take the opposing lawyers' side when clients express disagreement or reservation with their attorney's statements. I will say in sharp tones: "Excuse me for interrupting but your lawyer is trying to help you. You have no reason to talk in that manner." My legal opponent perceives I am sympathetic that he has to deal with an unpleasant client. The client starts to act like a kicked dog without a friend in the room. It is an attempt to build an ally and create doubts between the nasty client and the opposing lawyer.

Another tactic I use is to give a dismissive look at the other lawyer, a derisive glance that I know his client will notice and remember. My hope is that the lawyer's client will think that the point his attorney made had no merit.

The canons of legal ethics prohibit an attorney from communicating with the opposing client. All communication must be exclusively lawyer to lawyer. But sometimes a lawyer can communicate a subtle message to an opposing client—if it falls within ethical considerations. Here's an example: In a settlement conference, lawyer A listens to the argument of lawyer B. But when A talks about the case, lawyer B pays no attention and perhaps looks at unrelated papers during the talk. Rude? Perhaps. But it sends message to A's client that his lawyer is not worth listening to.

If I can drive a wedge of doubt on one point, I may be able to increase the confidence gap between the other lawyer and client. But the receptivity level to my client's position may also rise if my adversaries have to spend time and energy mollifying their nervous Nelly. They will be less attentive to the details of the case, and my dismissive look and inattention may have created a distraction that I can use to my purpose.

In some divorce conferences, one party may become upset, even teary. The visible emotion is distracting to the lawyer, who must interrupt the discussion to comfort a distraught client. Their focus on the case wavers and is diffused. If I see the other client is crying or upset, I tend to be oversolicitous. I say, "Let's take a break. Can I bring you a glass of water, coffee, or tea?" I have established a good communication with the tearful one and have demonstrated that I am a decent person, not an ogre.

COMMON ADVERSARIES

Have you heard the old saw, "Why do grandchildren and grandparents get along so well? Because they share a common enemy—parents."

When dealing with adversaries, common sense suggests that everyone should be situated on the same side of the table for as many issues as possible. One strategy to accomplish this goal is to create an out-of-the-room enemy. This tactic will convert adversaries into partners and can speed up the negotiation for overall agreement.

In negotiations, it is easy to make the Internal Revenue Service a mutual enemy. At the start of discussions, I say, "How we can make Uncle Sam pick up some of the cost of this?" I am not talking about doing anything illegal or unethical but about structuring a deal to obtain the best tax treatment, an appropriate enterprise and one that is part of a lawyer's duty to his client.

In a recent divorce case, the couple's assets had been reduced, owing to the poor performance of their stock portfolio. As the discussions continued over time, the pie of marital assets kept shrinking. At the commencement, we would have accepted a fair share of the assets for the nonworking wife without need for spousal maintenance. But months later, after a disastrous downturn in the market, any future tax-free income from her settlement—from even the safest investments—could not meet the wife's minimum financial needs. I had to ask for maintenance, citing the decline in the stock market. The husband and his attorney agreed that the request represented an equitable solution. The falling stock market was the bad guy, the common enemy, and the deal was made before the market declined further.

We had a similar situation in a declining real estate market where the couple had to sell their marital home as part of the settlement. Both wanted to obtain the highest possible price and rushed to put the house on the market. Bankruptcy represents another situation where it may be wise to end the case before complicating and unsettling financial factors come into play.

I have experienced cases where the husband pleaded guilty to a crime and wanted to resolve his wife's divorce claim before he went to jail. An early settlement would guarantee her monies before the court imposed a large fine that would come out of available marital funds.

I had one occasion where the husband, who was about to plead guilty to a white-collar crime, gave substantial assets to his wife in a divorce case. He then went to jail for several years. I was chagrined to see him some years later driving across Manhattan in a Rolls-Royce convertible. I had the unworthy thought that although the breakup of the marriage was real, husband and wife colluded in protecting the money. I suspected they did not tell the lawyers the truth, and what the husband did was park his money with the wife while he was in jail. On release from prison, he asked for and received his share.

UNDERESTIMATING ADVERSARIES

The question to ask is, Does your opponent know more than you do? Or do you *perceive* that he knows more than you, which brings us to the same place. But disproving this opinion will take place in an actual contest, and only then will the truth emerge.

In my legal career, one of the most egregious instances of underestimating an opponent occurred while I was serving as a Federal Prosecutor. The Department of Justice in Washington, D.C., through the U.S. Attorney in the Eastern District of New York, prepared a vast conspiracy indictment. It lumped together Federal Housing Association (FHA) frauds encompassing builders, appraisers, and owners in an area called Mill Basin in Brooklyn, New York. I had looked at the indictment before it was served, and it seemed to me that it did not spell out a cause of action under the federal criminal law, that is, a federal crime. There was no question that there had been wrongdoing, but in criminal law a person must violate a particular statute in a particular way to be found guilty.

The authorities arranged an elaborate arrest of the defendants on Saturday. The federal government likes to arrest people on a Saturday because the people arrested stay in jail until Monday and have a long weekend to consider their plight. And there are the inevitable photographs in the Sunday papers of handcuffed defendants who have not yet been formally charged with any crime.

A minor player in the Mill Basin case hired a Court Street lawyer. He was not from the group of well-known lawyers who practiced criminal law or tried federal criminal cases in Brooklyn, but was a local Brooklyn-based business lawyer for this defendant. The attorney made a motion to dismiss the indictment. It was granted on the terms that I predicted; a specific violation of federal law was not spelled out in the government's papers. This fiasco, which proved to be a major embarrassment to the United States Attorney General, occurred because the government underestimated a small-time Court Street practitioner in Brooklyn.

Another case of judicial overconfidence occurred during the time Ed Koch was mayor of New York City. His administration decided to "clean up" the city of streetwalkers. The plan called for policewomen dressed in plain clothes to play-act the roles of prostitutes.

As soon as men ("the Johns") solicited the decoyed policewomen, they were arrested. Using photographs and wire recordings of the bust, the District Attorney (DA) had an airtight case against the men.

The defendants' lawyers instructed their clients to plead guilty. Only my friend Mel Sachs, a noted criminal attorney, urged his client not to take a plea—he insisted on a jury trial.

In court, the Manhattan District Attorney believed it had an open and shut case. The DA called the decoyed policewoman to the stand who testified the defendant offered her money for sex. When Sachs cross-examined her, he asked one question, "Are you a police officer or a prostitute?"

Her indignant answer was, "I am a police officer."

Then, Sachs moved for immediate dismissal of the case pointing out to the judge that the law prohibited solicitation of a "prostitute." His client had solicited an admitted "policewoman," not covered in the statute and not unconstitutional. Case dismissed.

Overestimating an Opponent

Overestimating an adversary is as serious as underestimating an opponent. Some years ago, the name Marvin Mitchelson bespoke legal magic. He was a lawyer from California, and he was the most sought-after name for the rich or the famous seeking divorces in the United States. Seemingly, like Superman, he leaped from one victory to another. In 1963, he argued *Douglas v. California,* which resulted in the United States Supreme Court stipulating that every defendant had a right to free counsel in the appellate process.

However, his best-known case, *Marvin v. Marvin,* was more publicity than result. Michelle Triola was the live-in lover of the actor Lee Marvin. She never married him but nevertheless had taken Marvin's name. She sued the actor under the theory of palimony and Mitchelson represented her in this publicized case. What everyone forgets is that Mitchelson lost. He returned to court, and the court said in substance, "In case you did not understand it, Mr. Mitchelson, you lost this case."

The case created the novel theory of palimony. A new legal industry began for lawyers who drew up "living-together" agreements. A man's fear was that if he had an affair with a woman and she moved in, later she could sue for palimony. It was considered advisable to draw up these palimony agreements as soon as possible in the relationship, preferably in the moments after the lights were turned out and before the two cigarettes twinkled in the dark.

The theory of palimony was based on an implied contract. For several years, the highest award of palimony in the United States was a case that I won. I represented a French actress against a New York man. Because of the diversity in citizenship, it ended up in federal court. The couple had a verbal agreement stipulating that the man had purchased a "handyman's special" fixer-upper apartment to be decorated by the live-in girlfriend. After restoration, it was to be sold and the proceeds divided. The girlfriend spent the next years shopping, decorating, and making it into an attractive place, and it was sold for about $800,000. But then the swine said, "Too bad, it's my apartment," and refused to share the monies from the sale with the girlfriend.

We went to court before Judge Edward Weinfeld, who was the oldest, acting federal judge in the United States. He was in his 90s and looked like a cadaver. But he still possessed all his faculties. He was astute and never took a note. At trial, I enumerated the involvement of my client, describing in detail the work she did—hiring contractors, supervising the work, buying the shades, matching the wallpaper, choosing the flooring, and so forth. We won a verdict worth about $400,000 to my client, the highest award ever at that time.

Subsequent to this case, huge verdicts in palimony have ensued. In the MagLite case, the inventor of the popular flashlight line dumped his live-in companion. She alleged that she helped him develop the idea of the MagLite and aided him in all aspects of his professional life from the beginning years of poverty and struggle to his later enormous wealth. At the end of the trial, she was awarded millions of dollars. The trial was seen on television, and what struck viewers was the visible sadness of this once loving couple, who needed a publicized trial to terminate the relationship.

MERRICK AND MITCHELSON

Marvin Mitchelson became a household word in the United States, in part because he was a genius at self-promotion. He would obtain a default judgment in a case and then newspapers would carry it because of the huge sum of money involved. He bragged about the verdict, but the smart money bet that these sums would never be collected.

I liked Mitchelson and found him charming socially. But professionally, he was unfocused; he consumed fame and notoriety like an illegal substance, always, like Icarus, flying too close to the sun. He went to federal prison for a time and was disbarred. After completing his sentence, his law license was returned. He is now in his seventies and is attempting to resurrect his law career.

David Merrick produced hit after hit after hit. I remember walking down West Fourty-Fifth Street and seeing on one side of the street or the other, *Subways for Sleeping, Funny Girl,* and *Stop the World, I Want to Get Off.* His success culminated in the boff hit *42nd Street.* After the show first received bad out-of-town reviews, he bought out the other backers' shares and then owned 100 percent of the musical. *42nd Street* became hugely profitable, with productions in London, Las Vegas, and even a revival in New York. The money tumbled in.

I had represented his third wife, Etan Merrick in her divorce from the showman. Then he married a fourth wife Karen Prunczik, who played Anytime Annie in the original company of *42nd Street.* Merrick hired me to represent him in a divorce case against Karen and in a conservatorship proceeding.

In old age, Merrick had a stroke and was taken to the hospital. After he escaped in his wheelchair, a police officer found him in a Chinese noodle factory and brought him back to the hospital. As a result of the stroke and his bizarre behavior, Karen, the current wife, attempted to become the conservator of his estate and replace Mort Mitofsky, Merrick's lifelong friend.

I asked Merrick why he hired me since I had been his adversary in the Etan divorce case. As best as I could understand since his speech was slurred from the stroke, he said I did so well against him that he wanted to use me this time against his present wife. One time I asked him why he had married Karen. (She was a capable tap dancer, but I thought she was quite plain.) I said to Merrick: "You could have succeeded with any beautiful girl in the world. Why marry this one?" He replied, "If I marry an unattractive woman, other men never try to take her away from me."

Karen Merrick hired Marvin Mitchelson, who was then at the top of his game. Presiding was an ornery, older judge named Hilda Schwartz. She once had a case involving a homeless man who was taken to Bellevue Hospital. He had diabetes and the doctors said his leg needed to be amputated to save his life, but he refused the operation. In such circumstances, a state supreme court judge convenes court on the hospital's premises and decides the degree of control a patient will have over treatment in life and death or amputation procedures. Two doctors testified that removing the man's leg was a medical necessity to save his life. The patient refused, and Judge Schwartz sided with the man. Two months later, the man walked out of the hospital with both his legs. This episode represented less than medicine's shining hour, but it reflected on Judge Schwartz's character.

The *Merrick v. Merrick* trial began and the first event that happened was Mitchelson, through another lawyer, asked to be admitted for the case *pro haec vice*. This is a legal mechanism whereby an out-of-state lawyer can come into a specific jurisdiction for a particular case. The process is for the visitor to ask for temporary admission to the Bar under the sponsorship of a lawyer in that state. When the question arose, I said to the judge, "I have no objection and support his admission *pro haec vice*." The judge admitted Mitchelson into the case based on my in-court sponsorship. No sooner was Mitchelson approved, when he moved to disqualify *me*. Even he was a little embarrassed and made some weak joke to the judge to cover his uneasiness. The basis of Mitchelson's motion to disqualify me was that I was representing Merrick in his divorce case and this created a conflict in the conservatorship case. The judge looked at him with anger and denied the request.

Mitchelson brought up some points, and in what must be the California legal manner, he sat in his chair behind the counsel desk while addressing the judge. Judge Schwartz said: "I do not know what the practice is in California but here in New York, lawyers stand when addressing the court." Mitchelson then stood up to continue the argument. Five minutes later, he rose to make an objection, and the judge turned to him all milk and honey in her voice and said, "Mr. Mitchelson, you do not have to stand up all the time. Please, sit down." This went on for about 40 minutes. "Stand up." "Sit down." "Stand up." "Sit down." Poor Mitchelson was at wit's end, not knowing whether to stand or sit. This was the judge's payback for Mitchelson's attempt to disqualify me moments after I had supported his request to be admitted to the New York Bar.

The trial was not going well for Mitchelson or Mrs. Merrick, and a settlement was suggested. During the lunch break in the trial, the lawyers and the litigants went back to my office uptown. We were supposed to return to court by 2 o'clock. Intense negotiations ensued. Merrick was seated in my office with Mort Mitofsky and friends. Mitchelson and Mrs. Merrick were in my conference room, and I went from room to room like Dr. Kissinger involved in shuttle diplomacy.

Karen, my superefficient secretary, churned out draft after draft with changes after changes. (Years later, Mayor Guiliani praised her fast shorthand and typing because she was one of the few secretaries who could keep up with his rapid pace). In what I thought was a strange request, Mitchelson wrote a personal note to Merrick asking him to autograph one of the copies of the agreement for him to keep as a memento. When I brought the request to Merrick, he ripped up the note and threw it on the floor.

As the negotiations continued, Judge Schwartz kept tele-phoning to insist that we return to court. I suspected her urgency was driven by the fact that the press was congregating in the courtroom. The media had covered the trial with interest, and she may have been playing to the reporters, who complained and pressed her about deadlines.

We reached an understanding of settlement and rushed down-town to the court. It was now the latter part of the afternoon on a hot New York summer's day. Eight people squeezed into Merrick's limousine, some sitting on laps. Merrick sat scrunched in the cor-ner, sweating and glowering under his toupee.

Mitchelson tried to lighten the somber mood by telling this appalling joke: "The Pope thought it was time for him to experi-ence the joys of sex with a woman. One of his advisors said, 'Fa-ther, she may recognize you.' The second advisor said, 'Blindfold her.' The first argued, 'But, Pontiff, she could recognize your voice.' The second answered, 'We'll stuff cotton in her ears.' Another advi-sor said, 'Pontiff, she could put her hands on your face and recog-nize these features.' The second suggested, 'We'll tie her hands.' And then the Pope spoke, 'I appreciate all the consideration for my papal privacy but there's only thing I want to know . . . does she have big t—ts?'" The joke went over like a lead balloon. Merrick scowled, his little black eyes glowering at Mitchelson. The joke was so outlandish, so out of place, so outré that the trip continued in silence until we arrived at the courtroom.

The lesson I learned from the Mitchelson experience was not to overestimate an adversary. He came to New York clothed with publicity that proclaimed he was the best lawyer in the country, and perhaps he even believed his press clippings. But in court, he had feet of clay. He was not insightful nor did he present cogent arguments. Perhaps I should have anticipated this, but remember I thought he was the fastest legal gun in the country.

Some years later, I had another client come to me who had at first consulted with Mitchelson. The case was complex, and it would have been difficult to reach a settlement, let alone achieve any favorable results. I thought the best course was to take a pass on it and tell the client I could not help her. I was shocked to learn that Mitchelson took the case, surprised that he would have the time, energy, and staff to undertake the preparation. It turned out to be a fiasco. Mitchelson did not satisfy the client, and the case ended with controversy.

Another case where I overestimated a lawyer involved the great Louis Nizer. I had an unusual case, comparable to one Nizer had written about in his excellent books. I called his office to ask for the briefs and transcript in that case because he had achieved a brilliant result. Lawyers do cooperate with each other, and his secretary sent me the briefs and the minutes in the case. When I read the minutes, it turned out it was not Nizer who had made the excellent motions, arguments, and pleadings; it was an associate in the office. Nizer adapted what had occurred in the firm's case and took the credit for its substance and inventiveness. After this incident, when I negotiated against Nizer, I regarded him without such reverential awe. He had even grander stature as a writer, but he was not as clever a lawyer as he publicly claimed.

ELIMINATING COMPETITORS

Some people believe that one way to gain an advantage is to eliminate the top negotiators on the other side. Or, if the option exists, to select someone else who can be beat. In any field, there exists a small group of outstanding and skilled people. Most of life is similar to the Major League baseball's annual batting averages; people fit into a bell-shaped curve where the average person hits .270 year after year. Very few break the .300 barrier, and fewer still hit over .300.

When I first started private practice, specializing in matrimonial law, I took offices in the same building with a much publicized and feared divorce attorney named Irving Erdheim. Since few attorneys practiced this kind of law, a legitimate tactic by a man starting divorce proceedings was to visit me on the 11th floor and then go see Erdheim on the 20th floor or vice versa. These back-to-back consultations meant that neither of us could represent the man's wife. The rules of law and ethics had eliminated competition.

I have had variations on this theme played against me and have been the victim of this trick a few times over the years. I had to withdraw a case because it turned out that although I was representing the husband, the wife had consulted me 12 years earlier. I had no record of it but the woman produced a canceled check. She had sought my advice to disqualify me from ever representing her husband and safeguarded the check, which she showed as proof of our earlier meeting.

Removing Luminaries

Like other lawyers in the field, I do not talk on the telephone with people who want to make an appointment. If I am not hired—and later there is litigation—it never fails that the callers claim they told me every intimate detail of their lives on the telephone, therefore prohibiting me from representing the spouse. I have always made it a point never to speak to potential clients who want to make an appointment.

Not long ago, a major industrialist came to see me about a breakup with his wife. I was surprised he consulted me because I represented his first wife. He told me a rambling story that had nothing to do with his marital affairs nor did he seek any advice. He handed me a check at the end of our conversation. Soon after, his second wife asked me for divorce representation but I realized

I could not be her attorney because of the husband's prior consultation. His actions were calculated and successful.

Today my staff is cautious, keeping records of all people who have come to see us, going years back. The problem in New York City, as in any major urban area, is that we encounter an unlimited number of Thomases, Cohens, Schwartzes, Lees, and Jenkins. We try to obtain a first name and an address, or at least a telephone number, to verify whether we have ever seen that person before.

I had a case involving an English actor who became a citizen of a canton in Switzerland. A standard move for British actors to avoid high U.K. taxes was to become residents of one of the Bahamian islands or Switzerland. I told this actor that one street in a particular city in the Swiss canton housed all the divorce lawyers. I instructed him to visit all 16 lawyers on the street and tell his story. His wife would have to go to another canton or another Swiss city to obtain the services of an attorney. I knew that in Switzerland it was better to have a local lawyer for representation and not an attorney from another region. Out of the 16, the actor told me he was able to see 15, paying each one a consultation fee. He failed to consult the last one, who was out of the office on a skiing holiday. The end of the tale is obvious; the wife ended up hiring local lawyer number 16 and the husband's 15 paid consultations came to naught.

SMARTS

When I first heard the tragic news about record tycoon Phil Spector and the deadly shooting in his gated California house, I called Jerome's son and daughter to ascertain if they still kept in touch with Spector, who had once been my brother's close friend.

I was not a friend of Spector, but he had enjoyed a long friendship with Jerome. Spector flew into New York for my brother's funeral and was a speaker at the Rock and Roll Hall of Fame when Jerome was posthumously inducted.

Spector's name was flashed around the country when an actress was shot to death at his home. I wanted to know if my nephew and niece had been in touch with Spector because I thought I could give him an entrée to first-class California lawyers that he might not otherwise have enjoyed. I indicated that if he was guilty, Johnnie Cochran was the best choice, and if innocent, Robert Shapiro would be the best lawyer. Without any input from me, as it turned out, Spector chose Shapiro. This was the kind of case where a lawyer's remarks come into play. Shapiro never grandstanded the case in front of the press, never issued self-serving media statements, never went on television declaring his client's innocence or stating the district attorney did not have a case. He never raised the prosecutor's hackles by seizing the limelight in front of the public and embarrassing the authorities.

Later, Spector announced that he was not going to be indicted, and this statement created antagonism. I was concerned that his declaration would force an indictment by the DA's office when otherwise there would not have been one. Spector was not indicted, closing that chapter on a case well handled by Robert Shapiro.

There is yet another interesting postscript to this case involving Marvin Mitchelson, who was a friend of Spector and made himself available to the press. Spector was the subject of a long interview in *Esquire*, in which he condemned Mitchelson for violating their friendship and spouting off to the media. Mitchelson, charming as he may be, put his foot in his mouth—again.

Spector related an anecdote when my brother Jerome was inducted into the Rock and Roll Hall of Fame. My brother lived in the Consulate Hotel, which was located across the street from the Brill Building, the heart of Tin Pan Alley. The Brill was an 11-floor office building, and every floor had music publishers and song-writers in cubicles. Pianos sounded day and night with the tune-smiths hoping to land a big hit on the charts. A visitor would pass a door that said Bing Crosby Music or Perry Como Music. Jerome signed with a company called Hell and Range Music.

The Consulate was once called the Hotel Forest, home to an ill-fated event. The leading clown from Barnum & Bailey Circus, then appearing at the old Madison Square Garden on Eighth Avenue, stayed at the hotel for the circus's New York run. He had returned to the hotel with a prostitute who beat him to death with a fire extinguisher. The sordid incident took the bloom off the Forest Hotel's good name, and it was changed to the Consulate.

On the first floor of the Consulate was a steakhouse called Joe Marsh's Spindletop. The stated owner was Joe Marsh, but the rumors flew that the real owner was Meyer Lansky's son-in-law. The infamous Lansky was supposed to have been the brains behind organized crime in the United States, controlling gambling and other illicit operations in Las Vegas and Cuba. Lee Strasberg played the Lanksy-like character in *Godfather: Part II.*

Spector explained that when he visited my brother, Jerome invited him to the Spindletop. While they were having dinner, two tables away a man walked over to one of the diners, put a gun in the man's ear, and blew his brains out. Spector became very agitated and was upset the rest of the evening.

Months later, when Spector called Jerome to announce he was returning to New York, my brother suggested eating at the Spindletop.

Spector objected, "I can't go to that restaurant. Two tables away a man had his head blown off."

Jerome asked, "Phil, was the steak good?"

Phil said, "Yeah."

My brother continued, "Was the owner nice to you?"

"Yeah."

My brother said, "Was the service good? The staff nice to you?"
"Yeah."

My brother said, "So there was *one* bad part. Let's go there again for dinner."

ANTAGONISTIC PARTIES

Divorce is unpleasant for both parties. Robert Louis Stevenson wrote, "Marriage is like life in this—that it is a field of battle, and not a bed of roses." By the time couples reach the divorce lawyer's offices, the bed of roses resembles a bed of thorns.

I never know the depths of hate that clients feel for each other until the first meeting when I see husband and wife together in the same room. Time and again, this represents the couple's first face-to-face encounter since the day one person walked out of the shared living quarters. The scene is fraught with tension and hostility, particularly, if one spouse cheated on the other. I schedule this initial meeting in my conference room, which has a long, thick table that keeps the divorcing parties at a safe distance.

A divorce corresponds to a breakdown. It represents great stress to everybody. It is an admission of failure because divorce signals a message that people made a mess of an important part of life, their marriage. With failure comes anger, and people refuse to admit failure; it is almost always the other spouse's fault. But deep down, divorcing parties recognize that they bear some of the responsibility. At first this terrible anger is diffused, then it settles on the spouse, and in the last hostile stage, it is transferred to the spouse's lawyer.

The goal of divorce is to allow the parties to move on with their lives by settling the financial problems. But on frequent occasions, that settlement is not the goal of one spouse or the other; instead it is revenge, and with raw vengeance sometimes comes the desire to humiliate the other spouse in public.

In *Moby Dick*, Herman Melville wrote, "He heaped upon the white whale's hump all the hatred and rage that had been in his race since Adam down." Often I feel that litigants in divorce are filled with pent-up rage that they hope to rain down on the opposite side.

In the thorny Mia Farrow and Woody Allen custody proceedings, the public witnessed the lower depths of odium that one person could feel for another. In custody cases, each side attempts to amass negative characteristics to build a basis for denying the other party custody. In the trial for custody of their biological son, Satchel (later renamed Seamus), Farrow accused Allen of fondling their adopted daughter, Dylan.

I felt empathy for Allen's lawyer, Elkan Abramowitz, because once this repugnant charge was dropped into the trial, it became a runaway train that no amount of expert testimony could stop. It mattered little that in the end Allen was cleared of these repulsive charges. By inference, the public will assume he was guilty of something. I commented about Allen and his new wife Soon-Yi when I said, "I think they are a little like the Duke and Duchess of Windsor. They are trapped with each other, and they will forever be drifting together through time."

Often a case explodes because the husband or wife acts with marked antagonism. In the much-publicized Ronald Perleman divorce case against his wife, Patricia Duff, he played by the rules, but she behaved badly by hiring and firing one lawyer after another. I declined to be in this revolving door group. The public soon tired of her shenanigans but not the media, which kept a running scorecard of the revolving-door lawyers.

Unseen Harm

A public divorce case with a big movie star demonstrates how reckless philandering can embarrass and humiliate a party in a failed marriage. My client was Iolanda Quinn, wife of Academy Award winner Anthony Quinn. She was a charming woman who loved life with the virtue and grace associated with times long past. She was an Italian who spoke English with a slight accent. At the time of the trial, she was sixty-two, but could have passed for a woman 20 years younger. She was the mother of three children and had devoted her 31-year marriage to husband and family. Quinn, on the other hand, had been a serial adulterer who, at age eighty-two, fathered two children with thirty-five-year-old Kathy Benvin, his former secretary. It was believed that the priapic actor had a total of 13 children from two wives and three girlfriends.

The press had a field day with the Quinn-Benvin May–December relationship, writing reams of pap about the siring of children by an octogenarian. At the annual Academy Awards, with the whole world watching, emcee Billy Crystal quipped, "Women who win tonight receive an Oscar. The losers can have a baby by Anthony Quinn." Larry King, in an on-air interview, lauded the actor as "The Mighty Quinn."

Quinn's philandering was a front-page story in Italy. Poor Iolanda had to face the paparazzi and their barrage of humiliating questions whenever she returned to her native country.

When the case came to trial, I proceeded on the grounds of egregious fault. In a divorce case, fault does not affect establishing the percentage of equitable distribution unless one can prove that actions in the marriage produced horrifying results. If proved, the court will award a kind of punitive damage to the settlement.

An example of egregious fault was a case in New Jersey where the husband hired a hit man to murder his wife. Another case involved a husband who stabbed his spouse 12 times. Incest cases also fall into this harm category. And another case saw a wife lying to the police, who removed her husband from his law firm in handcuffs.

My argument was that Quinn committed uniquely cruel acts to Iolanda. He made life a living hell by the humiliation he caused her, especially when she returned to Italy for family visits. The bitter end of the marriage with his new fatherhood presented a clear example of an egregious fault.

Barry Slotnick, a criminal lawyer, was my opponent in the Quinn case. He had enjoyed his 15 minutes of fame representing Bernard Goetz in the notorious shooting of four teenagers on a New York City subway in 1984. After *Goetz*, Slotnick appeared on television almost any time there was a major criminal case in New York. But I had kept tabs on his performance and noticed that he seemed to have lost the most serious cases. Even the bathrobe-clad mobster Vincent "Chin" Gigante replaced him.

Criminal lawyers occasionally will take on matrimonial cases if their calendar is not full, or sometimes even when it is. In Florida, when drug trafficking cases dried up, some lawyers turned to divorce cases. One might posit that crimes against the heart have a kinship with crimes that violate the statutes.

Slotnick sports a full beard, which seems to change color by his whim or by the changing of the seasons. Over time, friends reported that people had mistaken him for me. He was unhappy that, despite his former frequent television appearances, he was wrongly identified as Felder, the Bearded One. In fact, one newspaper printed a "Separated at Birth" column that featured our bearded profiles side by side (like the Smith Brothers cough drop package). Another newspaper ran a story about our feud (untrue) that Slotnick framed and placed on his office wall.

I was unimpressed by Slotnick's performance during the Quinn case. I thought that his extensive criminal law experience would come into play during the trial but I soon realized his work was quite ordinary. I conducted a *voir dire*, which involves cross-examining the fundamentals of what the witness will offer into evidence to permit the judge to admit the testimony or to refuse it.

He seemed at sea over my questioning. In addition, he served me papers that I recognized contained sections taken from papers for one of my prior cases. He had hired a person formerly in my employ, who subsequently hired herself out to other lawyers on a per diem basis. Obviously, unbeknownst to Slotnick, she took the work product as a sample of her knowledge and used it word for word in assisting Slotnick.

In court, Slotnick charged that Iolanda was a true abuser in the long marriage. He further asserted that she told lies to win more than 90 percent of Quinn's multimillion-dollar estate. It was the wrong tack. The truth for everyone to see was that Quinn brutalized Iolanda and had walked out of the marriage of his own volition and then fathered two children with another woman.

Slotnick did not realize, or did not appreciate, that a lawyer cannot throw out theories without facts to back up the assertion. To set the record straight, I called to the stand their son, thirty-three-year-old Danny Quinn. He was an honest, forthright young man who loves his father but accused him of abusing Iolanda by hitting her and shouting obscenities. In researching my book about spousal abuse, *Getting Away with Murder*, I recognized that Quinn's victimization of Iolanda fit into the classic abuse pattern. In court, no one, except maybe Slotnick, believed Quinn was a victim. Everyone sympathized with Iolanda for the years of cruelty she had endured. Quinn settled before the trial went further.

The moral of the story is that adversaries are like wine in a bottle. Often what looks like a great vintage, turns out to be sour to the taste. It is always best not to overestimate or underestimate an opponent.

UNDERSTANDING
THE PACE

S peaking about cigars, and explaining why cigar smokers
wave a match around the end of a cigar before lighting up,
Winston Churchill said, "You have to warm a woman before you assault her." Negotiations are like lighting a cigar.
Finding the right tempo, whether in lovemaking or negotiation, is
a matter of pacing.

The pace of negotiations varies with time and place and substance. If I have a case in Manhattan with other New York
lawyers, I know that the drive for resolution will be somewhat
fast. But if I am dealing with an English law firm or with clients
from the Middle East, time becomes an ancillary and less important variable in the mix.

Each negotiation sets its own rhythm, and many factors affect it. Some variables may be personal, such as an individual's
stamina. Others, like an impending snowstorm, are beyond
anyone's control. The eventual pace will play out, but the trick
is to know ahead of time how long it will take to reach a final
conclusion.

Your Internal Clock

Internal rhythms help determine the tempo of negotiations. I always have required only three or four hours of sleep, and when I first started practicing law, I would not feel tired in the late evening. My ability to stay up past midnight and beyond was an advantage in long deliberations.

My brother and I were both night owls. Jerome would doze on and off sitting up in his bed, wake up refreshed, and write best-selling hit tunes. The no-sleep champ, however, was the renowned Hasidic grand rabbi, Joel Teitelbaum of Brooklyn, who did not sleep in a bed in 25 years. He would fall asleep in his chair, catch a few hours of rest, wake up, and then continue to work.

Time Constraints and Deadlines

Time becomes an important variable in pacing negotiations. In legal discussions, we have no fixed time constraints. Judges (mainly, the old-timers) may order lawyers not to leave the courtroom without an agreement. Or, on occasion, judges will allow an additional 30 minutes or an hour to deliberate. The ticking of the clock alone cannot induce a final agreement, but time can set the pace. Setting a deadline can make adversaries nervous and anxious. With a time constraint, everyone wants to settle quickly, and even though items in the debate are far apart, time limitations may give you an advantage.

Decisions on Time

I advise clients to put off a decision about moving children to a new school until March or April. In the late spring, spouses and children become apprehensive as the deadline for next autumn's enrollment approaches. At that point, they will often negotiate a compromise that meets everyone's school objectives. It is unrealistic to begin school negotiations in the winter for the following September's admission.

Vacation plans represent an additional negotiation affected by time constraints. If you and your spouse or date cannot agree on a destination, a good delaying tactic is to ask to study the brochures of the other person's preferred vacation spot. Keep reading and analyzing the literature until the last moment when it is either go or no-go for the vacation. Perhaps the critical moment arises when you reach the deadline to purchase discounted airfares; then it is either book or pay a higher ticket tariff at a later date. At this juncture, start voicing approval of the other person's choice and also slip in a few mild negatives about the selection (e.g., "I'd love to fly down to romantic Poway Del Mar but it's jammed with Europeans camping and cooking bratwurst on the beach"). Continue with these discouraging facts always stressing your desire to go until the other person (perhaps, subconsciously) becomes hesitant and suggests a different vacation spot or, better, asks to hear your preferred selection. With time winding down, you must make a decision soon, or any trip will be impossible.

DEADLY DEADLINES

In 1974, a major industrialist whom I had represented was ill with a serious infection that the doctors predicted would soon end his life. The only possible hope rested with a now commonly used antibiotic that then had not yet received FDA approval. The drug was being tested in a limited experimental protocol and was unavailable to the public.

The client's children asked if I could find a way to have their father accepted for testing in the treatment program. My research revealed that a New Jersey branch of the pharmaceutical company that manufactured the drug was involved in the protocol. My phone calls to the company's headquarters generated negative responses, and even when I persisted in talking about life or death, I encountered an endless chain of bureaucratic buck-passing. One kind soul mentioned that the president of the drug company alone could circumvent the rigid protocol and, even then, only in the rarest of circumstances.

I obtained the man's name, which surprisingly was listed in an upper New Jersey telephone directory. When I reached him at home, I explained who I was and the dire straits that had precipitated my call, punctuating the conversation with facts relating to my client's worsening condition. The deadline was fast approaching for any last-minute attempt to save the man's life.

The company's president explained that his hands were tied; only those patients in the protocol could obtain the drug. No desperate pleading or cajoling on my part would change his decision. I had anticipated that response and played the one negotiating card I held—I offered cash. I proposed $1 million to the company or to the president's favorite charity with the promise of a certified check the following day. There was a pause, and then he said he would think about it overnight. The next morning he telephoned to say that he thought we could work something out.

The next day, however, my client's family found a doctor in Boston who had space for one additional patient in the protocol, and finally, the sick man obtained the drug. If he had ever learned of my cavalier behavior in offering $1 million of his vast fortune, he would have reproached me for throwing away his money.

Very rich people, even in regard to their own health, often behave like Scrooge, reluctant to part with a dime. Once earlier in a conversation, I asked the same man how he kept his good humor and spirits up while undergoing painful medical treatments. He said it was difficult and that he would give all his riches not to be so afflicted—but then he quickly corrected his words to say that to be cured of the illness, he would give *half* of his wealth.

A less dramatic example of a deadline involved Roy Cohen. I knew from years of socializing with Cohen and reading about him in the gossip columns that he was ardent New York Yankees fan, a friend of George Steinbrenner. A case reached the final day of negotiations and Cohen had mentioned the day before that he would like to settle so that he could attend an afternoon World Series game at Yankee Stadium.

I set the meeting in my office for 11:30 A.M., which would have given him time to review the case, resolve outstanding differences, and arrive at the stadium as Steinbrenner's guest for the opening pitch. I started the meeting on time. I took the time to review the finances in the case, which seemed legitimate since we were working with the same set of numbers. I then pretended that important detailed notes were missing from the case file. I exited the room, stating that I had to look for the notes (a not uncommon situation in a busy lawyer's office). Before returning to the room, I arranged with my secretary to call me out of the conference room in a few minutes to take a phone call from a judge in another case (false). After returning 20 minutes later, I again had to leave the conference room to take a long-distance call from England (false again).

Cohen started pacing the room, his anxiety about leaving increasing exponentially in response to the ticking of his internal clock. Every minute delayed meant the possibility of missing the start of the game. Each time I returned to the room, I apologized and emphasized how sympathetic I was since I sensed his urgency to finish the meeting and go to Yankee Stadium. These statements accentuated the time predicament. I chose a detailed section of the case to review that required drawn-out minutes of discussion.

"I'll sign," Cohen shouted, running out the door. "Prepare the papers and I'll sign!" I rode down in the elevator, and we signed the papers in the building's lobby. He was desperate to leave and gave up the case to make it in time for the opening pitch.

MIRON LUMBER COMPANY

Miron Lumber Company is a sprawling operation in the industrial section of Greenpoint, Brooklyn. I learned my first lessons in the art of pacing in negotiations when I accompanied my father there. In his 30 years of dealings with the owner of the company, I never knew the man's first name because my father simply called him "Miron" and he called my father "Felder."

Miron used my father as the company's lawyer from its earliest days when it was a small, one-man business. He was an immigrant—a hands-on, hard-knuckled, self-made businessman who regarded legal costs as a disagreeable but necessary expense. My father would save up the bills until money was short at home, and then we would make a trip to Greenpoint for collection.

From years of experience handling the account, my father knew that when he presented and explained a bill for legal services, Miron would respond with disbelief, shocked that someone was asking him for money. Miron reacted to the request for payment of legal fees like a man taking a sharp jab to the belly. The two men would then engage in a sort of a stylized Kabuki dance of demands and offers lasting an indeterminate length of time. They refined the ritual over the years, and Miron's sons, who worked in the business, and I were the silent onlookers at these meetings. We realized there would be no resolution without a formal beginning, middle, and end to these negotiations.

The two opponents began the dance when the men were in their mid-fourties, and it continued until they turned seventy. The negotiations began late in the day because both men thought that the other one would be fatigued and not up to his game. Each one freed up several hours at the end of the day to allow time for the discussions.

At first, there would be small talk about family life or the Brooklyn Dodgers; perhaps a glass of tea would be offered; and next they would discuss business in general. Miron would always complain that business was bad, ignoring the ever-expanding area the company occupied, the numerous trucks coming in and out of the yard (in full view of me and my father), and the telephones ringing with new orders. My father would indicate how busy he was, a celebration of fantasy over reality. After the fibs had been exchanged, my father would review the legal work he had done for the company, checking off items one by one on a yellow pad. As he enumerated each project, Miron's face grew paler and paler. The owner acted as though my father was a doctor reciting a long list of terminal ailments. I imagined that every legal item my father quoted rang up like a cash register sale in Miron's mind.

At the moment when my father finished his spiel, the histrionics began on both sides. Miron frequently feigned a heart attack or at least an attack of the vapors, requiring him to sit down and demand a glass of water. He complained that paying the bill would kill him, put him out of business, and force his family to stand on the breadline. What kind of lawyer was my father to charge a poor, working-class Brooklyn lumberman fancy-schmancy Manhattan prices?

My father, no slouch in the emotional behavior department, countered by ranting and raving about fair fees for services. And he would always reveal that he had started out in life as a veterinarian but had been forced to change careers midstream to put food on the table for his wife and two boys. Often, he would grab my arm and say, "Son, we're through here. Let's go." And out of the lumberyard, we went. Of course, Miron followed us into the street, shrieking, "There's no reason to act crazy." And, of course, we always returned.

The next stage of the negotiations witnessed Miron trying to shave off a few dollars from the bill. At this juncture, my father would shout, "If you don't think my services were worth the price, then pay me nothing." He would gather up his papers and made motions to bolt out the door. Back and forth the two men would bicker, Miron carping about the high expense and my father claiming his legal work was a bargain.

Exhausted, the pair would shake hands, agree on a fee, and finish the negotiations. The old men acted like aging prizefighters, slugging it out for the full 15 rounds in a bout that ended in a draw. Each side thought it had won, but I believe what each man enjoyed was the dance. Once the bargaining was over, they went back to a discussion of families and who in the neighborhood had died in the past year.

THE WILDENSTEIN DIVORCE

In 1998, I represented art dealer Alec Wildenstein in his acrimonious divorce from his wife Joycelyne. To respect confidentiality (although the proceedings often became a media circus), I will confine my comments to the portion of the case publicly reported in the press. I want to demonstrate how learning the behavior of one participant convinced me I was in for a time-consuming proceeding.

As reported in great detail in the media, the wife, Swiss-born Joycelyne Wildenstein, had been a classic beauty in her youth, as well as being athletic, multilingual, and an accomplished pilot. She traveled in the tony European jet set of the very rich. I presume she could have had her choice of wealthy European men but she fell in love with Alec Wildenstein. The European and American press stated that he was an aristocratic French-born,

American-educated scion of almost a 10-billion-dollar family fortune. The media vastly overexaggerated the sum. The Wildensteins were alleged to own the world's most important private family art collection.

The magazines reported that in 1978, love blossomed during a shooting weekend at Alec's 66,000-acre estate in Kenya, and they married soon after. The marital history would show that they produced two wonderful sons and for years seemed to be a lovingly devoted couple. The Wildensteins lived alternately in a huge estate outside Paris, the vast ranch in Africa, and a spacious New York East Side townhouse filled with breathtaking works of art. Court records and reported decisions, as reflected in the press and reported decisions—whether rightfully or inaccurately—stated that they spent $1 million a month to maintain their lifestyle. Alec, a devoted husband, lavished jewels on his wife; the reported value of the collection was estimated at $10 million.

The phrase from the seventeenth century that "Beauty's but skin deep" had an adverse effect on the marriage as Joycelyne, at the age of 50, began a futile attempt to maintain a youthful appearance. In a quirk of the psyche, she underwent a succession of plastic surgeries on her face that made her look like a wild jungle cat with slits for eyes and plump, puffy lips. The media enjoyed a field day reporting her bizarre appearance; New York Magazine showed her surgically altered leonine face on one of their covers and dubbed her, "THE BRIDE OF WILDENSTEIN."

In the beginning of the divorce proceedings, both Wildensteins (Alec most of all) acted with civility and courtesy. As a rule, divorce cases proceed smoothly when lots of money is on the table because vast wealth means neither party will have to give up a luxurious lifestyle. Among the very rich, there often is a mechanical division of assets. I knew that Alec was a European gentleman from the old school who would settle generous sums on his wife and children.

Seeing Joycelyne up close, and observing her subtle hostile behavior, made me wonder whether her early display of politesse was a sham. I began to doubt that the settlement would proceed amicably as I perceived she might set a pace that satisfied her desire to act out the victim's role in public (or any persona that could put her name and face in the limelight). In effect, her now disfigured face could be seen as a silent message to the public: "Look at what has happened to me. I am a woman to be pitied." I anticipated that she would take other aggressive steps to put a spin on the dissolution of the marriage and to depict Alec as a callous husband who had discarded a faithful spouse.

To be truthful, I failed to gauge the depth of her anger and was not prepared for the midnight assault on Alec's privacy (although the media had been tipped off). One night, Joycelyne and two private bodyguards stormed into Alec's bedroom in their townhouse (owned by his family). According to the press, they allegedly discovered him *in flagrante delicto* with a young, blonde Russian beauty. Alec, when faced with strangers in his bedroom, assumed with good reason that thieves had broken into the house. He brandished a licensed, nine-millimeter pistol. The police arrived soon after and arrested him. Alec dressed for the handcuffed ride downtown to night court in an Armani suit, silk shirt, and tie. The *New York Daily News* headline the next day blared the night's events: "A WIFE, A TEEN LOVER, A GUN."

Alec was placed in the Tombs, the notorious Manhattan jail to await arraignment. After receiving his middle-of-the-night telephone call, I rushed to the courthouse, fearing that the Park Avenue Alec would be an easy mark for the degenerate scum that the criminal justice system had sucked up during the night and locked in the same holding pen. But when I reached the cell, I found him undamaged, not a hair out of place, and looking, for all intents and purposes, like a man selecting a chateau bottled estate wine from a four-star restaurant.

At the arraignment, Alec was charged with three counts of second-degree menacing and released on his own recognizance. No bail was required. I returned to the holding pen to see if he had left any personal objects. There, the police officer on duty said, "If strangers had burst into my bedroom in the night, I would have shot them."

I asked if he had witnessed what happened when Alec was led into the cell filled with the night's dregs and druggies. I was curious why none of the lowlife had mussed a hair on Alec's head.

"Yeah, I saw it," the policeman replied, "The scumola asked Mr. Wildenstein what he was in for."

"What did he answer?"

"I think he said that he shot someone. Maybe he said, 'I shot my wife.'"

In Manhattan, this is a good reason to keep hands off a cellmate, even if he is a classy gent in the same holding tank in the Tombs.

Joycelyne's ambush closed the door to a swift, amicable, and private divorce settlement. I always believed that her sudden arrival with private detectives to the townhouse that night was a setup. It was John Dos Passos who wrote in *Great Days*, "It's the wrong choice, the slip o' the will that opens the door to disaster." Joycelyne Wildenstein would soon learn the sad truism of her "slip o' the will." Because of Alec's generous nature, she probably would have done much better financially in the case if she had taken a gentler route.

The townhouse attack was a deliberate and hostile act that was inconsistent with a wife whose goal was to pursue a harmonious, fair, and quick settlement. Joycelyne wanted a fight, and we adjusted the tempo of the divorce to provide time to defend a full-blown marital slugfest. The resulting negotiations took a backseat to charges and countercharges that prolonged the process for more than a year.

In an odd twist, Joycelyne met and romanced a lawyer whom she encountered at the same hair salon and who apparently visited the same plastic surgeon. He also ended up looking feline. The *New York Post* carried their photographs on the front page under the punning headline, "HER MANE MAN."

A final, tangential public mention of the Wildenstein case occurred many years later. The judge who presided, Marylin Diamond, complained of death threats in the mail, and as a result of this epistolary terrorization, the police provided her with bodyguards. The police became suspicious because each time they withdrew her protection, she received another letter. Later, during the post 9/11 anthrax scare, she received a mysterious powder in the mail. It turned out to be Bisquick baking mix. The police searched her garbage and found the same baking mix inside. Since she sat on the Wildenstein case, my client, Alec, was placed on the list of possible suspects. (To some in the press, the key "suspect" was Judge Diamond herself.) I doubt that Alec Wildenstein even remembered this judge's name, but I am certain that he wrote no threatening notes. I would wager a huge sum of money that the debonair millionaire had never handled a box of Bisquick in his life.

In divorce cases, experienced lawyers know that the final monetary settlement will have a plus or minus 10 percent swing from the first number put out on the table. On some occasions when I know that it is time to settle the case, I have to deal with a recalcitrant client who insists on continuing the process, hoping to turn the screw in a little tighter. The tactic is to show how much this persistence in superfluous negotiations will increase my fee. This usually ends the bargaining.

The ABCs of Auctions

Auctions provide a fine example of using pace to an advantage. I used to buy a lot of art and I was a frequent attendee at Sotheby's and Christie's. Over time, I developed a few simple ploys that max-imized my chances of winning bids, often at a lower price. I call these "Felder's Three Rules of Auction Bidding"—but they work for other purchases as well.

First, attend an auction house on a weekday. The weekend is packed with people, some of them amateurs and sightseers out for an afternoon's entertainment. These "Looky Lous" have no inter-est in winning an object and will often disrupt your rhythm by making outrageous bids. Sometimes I will be outbid by well-heeled tourists who have no sense of the object's real value. The second rule is to make a habit of attending an evening auction and staying until the last item is displayed. Late at night, people are tired and want to go home. After 10 P.M., the room will start to thin out, leaving fewer bidders and increasing your chances for obtaining a bargain. The third rule to follow is, if possible, go to an auction when it's raining or when rain is predicted to start dur-ing the auction. In these three instances, you will find substan-tially fewer people and those in attendance are anxious to exit.

Telephone bidders at home do not experience the energy or drama of a spirited auction. Be wary of these electronic interlopers when bidding because they are removed from the reality of the auction and are unconscious of time. I visualize them stretched out on chaise lounges, popping bonbons with one hand, holding the telephone in the other, and tossing off bids while watching a soap opera.

Opponents' Idiosyncrasies

Learn the habits, the health, and even the idiosyncrasies of your opponents, and then use this information to promote a winning approach. This is true of a spouse or child or anyone with whom you have a frequent dialogue.

I represented a wife in a divorce case whose husband suffered from diabetes. I learned this fact by studying the court papers, which include a spouse's detailed health history because it could be a factor when computing future economic needs in a divorce case. The husband was insulin-dependent. I took full notice of his condition during some of the early meetings, observing that he required food at regular intervals to sustain a level of blood sugar.

When the negotiations reached the critical stage of deciding periodic and lump-sum payments, I scheduled the meeting of the lawyers and client for late in the afternoon. In past dealings, the husband had acted difficult and punitive, and had turned down our reasonable demands. As the hard bargaining negotiations dragged on, I could see that he was lapsing into lethargy. I realized that he needed food, and at his request, I telephoned in an order to a nearby restaurant.

When the food arrived, my secretary announced that the "UPS messenger" was at the front desk. This was a prearranged code that the food had arrived, and I stepped out of my office and moved to the receptionist. There I paid and tipped the delivery person and threw the food into a wastebasket of a nearby office. Negotiations proceeded, but I knew the husband's mind was elsewhere. I asked whether he wanted to end the meeting because the food order had not arrived. He agreed to wait a few more minutes, and I made a bogus call to the restaurant, acting irate at the long delay.

Then I telephoned another takeout restaurant. When the second delivery person arrived 30 minutes later, my secretary tipped me off that the "judge's papers" needed signing. I exited the conference room and repeated the payment and dumping routine. Over time, the husband's physical condition weakened, as did his resistance to our demands. Without the strength to continue arguing, he caved into our requests, which were more than fair and reasonable. The next morning, with his sugar stabilized, the husband may have wanted to change his mind.

I mentioned this case to Joyce Wadler in the "Boldface Names" column of the *New York Times*, adding now that I am older and mellower, I might suggest to a diabetic husband that he take his insulin. And I might even brew him a double latte with extra sugar.

British Affairs

In dealing with foreigners, I have learned that they are on a different time track. The dissimilarity occurs because of cultural differences in the way they do business; sometimes, with people of the Middle East, I think it is genetic. Be prepared for a long haul.

From time to time in my career, I have had to negotiate with British solicitors in transatlantic divorce cases. The agonizing truth is that these lawyers—among the highest paid in the world (Swiss attorneys, for some reason, seem to earn the most)—cannot finish a telephone call, let alone finish a case. The end is never in sight, and they apparently suffer from chronic abulia, a pathological inability to make a decision.

I was engaged in a lengthy case against Peter O'Toole, and one episode was played out in the British court. The court in London ruled in our favor, but I remember having telephone conversations with our London solicitor that had me pulling out what hair I had left because of the conversation's slow pace.

On my visits to London to discuss negotiations, the meetings with solicitors in the Temple often have taken on the appearance of a P.J. Wodehouse Bertie Wooster farce. I can understand the initial politeness, with inquiries about my flight and hotel accommodations. However, the conversations then continue with chitchat about the weather, an occasional offer to provide an introduction to their Saville Row tailor, talk about shows opening at the West End, transatlantic politics, and always, the leisurely serving of tea. Ironically, when I serve tea in my office, I brew a fresh pot with loose tea; but in London the *nouvelle vague* is to use tea bags. After 45 minutes of this small talk, the New York City time clock always begins ticking in my head reminding me that "time is money."

These British counselors-at-law also love to dawdle through overseas conference calls, even when they foot the pricey telephone bill. During conversations with eminent London jurists who have taken silk (i.e., been appointed Queen's counsel, a high honor), I have been able to put the telephone down and do paperwork on my New York desk while they prattled on in London.

Nevertheless, in questions of personal integrity, these solicitors are above reproach. When Mick Jagger was put under oath by telephone and allowed to testify in a New York proceeding while sitting in his lawyer's London offices, we were comfortable that it would be under the same constraints as if he appeared in person before the court in New York City.

A few London lawyers that I have dealt with could be transported to New York without terminal culture shock. Anthony Julius, the late Princess Diana's divorce lawyer, and his firm come prominently to mind. In fact, at a recent meeting in his new London offices, I was poured proper tea from a proper pot.

The Sands of Time

I would rather negotiate with a hundred tortoise-paced British lawyers than deal with one Middle Eastern client. When conferring with someone from the Arab world, one embarks on the proverbial slow camel trek across a desert of time. Arabs approach lawyers (and even each other when negotiating) with the anxious caution of two hyenas circling around leftover carrion.

Arabs are historically gracious when they invite you into their home or office. Culture necessitates that at first they never discuss money or business; it is considered impolite and inhospitable. Waiting for Arabs to begin negotiations is like waiting an eternity for an icicle to melt on a sunny day in the Arctic.

In the 1954 film *Beat the Devil*, with Humphrey Bogart and John Huston teaming up again, Bogie's character seeks to have hostages released from the clutches of a desert sheik. Inside the spacious tent, the Arab ruler shows no urgency in discussing the hostages or their plight. He enjoys all the time in the world, and slowly puffing on his water pipe, eyes half-closed in sensuous revelry, he asks the Bogart character, "Tell me about Rita Hayworth. Do you believe she would be interested in me?"

A classic film quote about time comes from this movie, which was scripted by Truman Capote. The Peter Lorre character says, "What is time? The Swiss manufacture it. The French hoard it. Italians squander it. Americans say it is money. Hindus say it does not exist. Do you know what I say? I say time is a crook."

One of my cases involved a Saudi Arabian woman who wanted a divorce from a wealthy Saudi husband. For reasons that I never understood, the husband's lawyer was based in Los Angeles. It was difficult to bring the parties together for negotiations. After almost a year of transcontinental paperwork with the California-based attorney, the husband and wife agreed to meet on the French Riviera for a final settlement discussion. I flew there expecting to resolve matters in a day. But again the Arab pastime of pleasure before business became apparent, and social activities took precedent. On the third day, we met aboard the husband's yacht and signed papers. Two New York lawyers could have accomplished these negotiations with a 15-minute phone call.

A case I turned down involved another rich Arab woman from Kuwait who asked me to represent her. We met in a large suite she maintained on a year-round basis at the Waldorf Towers, where an elegant servant greeted me at the door. As soon as we were seated, the man served me a plate of smoked salmon arranged in the shape of a Star of David, in the center of which was a mound of gefilte fish.

"I know you're a Jew," she said. "I wanted to make you feel at home with an Arab woman." I gave her a good grade for an attempt at honesty and ally building but bad marks for introducing the unessential into the conversation.

My interest in her case waned when I learned not only that I would have to fly to the Persian Gulf (this was prior to the Gulf War) for negotiations, but also that the wife's first lawyer had mysteriously disappeared after a prior meeting with the husband. I sensed that neither party was in a hurry to settle, and negotiations might drag on for months if not years.

A later divorce I considered was that of the native wife of a Saudi Arabian prince. We had to meet in London since her husband would not permit her to come to the United States, believing that I might commence an action in the U.S. courts even though they resided in Saudi Arabia. The prince feared an American judge would make a favorable ruling for her. Since he owned property in London, he was more comfortable with British courts deciding the case.

Our initial meeting in London was at the Dorchester Hotel, which was owned by Arabs. When I arrived for the appointment, servants were packing her bags because she did not like the suite's yellow color (Cecil Beaton yellow). We rescheduled after she was ensconced at the Ritz. The consultation was brief as I realized that U.S. courts had no jurisdiction over a native-born Arab domiciled in an Arab country. I eschewed a fee since the meeting lasted a scant 10 minutes. She insisted on giving me a token for my time (a gracious Arab gesture) and offered me an inert hand grenade from the Gulf War, which sits today on my office desk.

PATTER AND PACE

In preparation for a negotiation meeting, people will arrive with a scripted patter or set piece hoping to take control of the situation by reciting a practiced spiel. This pattern holds as true for attorneys in million-dollar negotiations as it does for children who seek to skip homework so that they can view an afternoon movie.

My best advice is to let opponents talk themselves out. Listening makes you wiser. Wait for adversaries to speak their piece. When they finish speaking, ask if they want to add more points to the discussion. In fact, nod your head attentively when they prattle on. Most people have little to say but will use a lot of words to say it. Sometimes, the less the substance, the more the words. When opponents have exhausted their presentation, move in for the kill.

Years ago in *Newsweek*, I wrote an article that was critical of Donald Trump's financial bailout plans. An understandably irate Trump telephoned me, beginning the conversation with "I thought [pointedly past tense] we were friends." After the opening fusillade, I let him talk on and did not interrupt his heated attack. Finally, his anger dissipated, "The Donald" hung up. Had I argued with him, it would have kept the fires of his displeasure burning. What was the point? The caveat is that time proved Trump and his bailout strategy were correct. He turned the corner and made a profitable recovery as a result of the economic times, his karma, skill, or all of the above. He bore me no ill will and since that time I have been a guest at his beautiful home in Palm Beach.

TIME STEALS INTENTIONS

Charles Forte, the British hotel magnate, lost the hotel chance of a lifetime in a negotiation by not knowing the pace. Lord Forte was the chairperson of Trusthouse Forte, one of the world's largest hotel and catering business, operating primarily but not exclusively in the United Kingdom. Starting with a modest milk bar in 1935, the ambitious Forte expanded operations through successful takeovers in Great Britain. By the 1960s, he had become that country's largest food supplier and a substantial hotelier as well.

In the 1970s, Trusthouse Forte expanded its operation in the United States by first managing Manhattan's Pierre Hotel. The group successfully reversed the hotel's $2.5 million loss per year into the generation of a $3 million profit. When the management lease ended, Forte could not convince the consortium of Pierre apartment owners (numbering over 100) to extend him a long lease.

The Pierre setback was short-term as Trusthouse Forte purchased the American-owned Knotts Hotel Corporation, which included the International Hotel at John F. Kennedy Airport and the prestigious Westbury and Mayfair hotels in New York City.

Forte was primed for the company's biggest coup, the purchase of the Plaza Hotel, the diamond in Manhattan's hotel crown. He would have succeeded save for a basic miscalculation: He did not realize the swift, urban pace of his unknown New York competitor, Sol Goldman. In a 1986 autobiography, Forte wrote:

> But I still remember bitterly the one that got away—the Plaza in New York. I had made an excellent offer of $22 million.

A Plaza hotel representative visited Forte, asking him to increase the bid to $22.5 million. For the extra amount, the hotel would be Forte's. The British magnate was so annoyed at the last-minute squeeze for an additional $500,000 that he decided to defer an answer until the next morning. Forte was in for a shocking surprise. As he wrote:

> On the following morning my New York solicitors rang to say that the hotel had been sold to someone else. . . . I had underestimated the man I was dealing with and had not realized how fast big business can be transacted, if necessary, in New York.

The one-night delay opened the door for Sol Goldman to grab the Plaza Hotel. Goldman was a seasoned veteran of the fast-paced New York real estate negotiations. He saw the window of opportunity open for a split second, and he made the Plaza deal without hesitation. For Sir Charles, the lesson was a painful one. He admitted:

> So, for a further $500,000 I had lost one of the most valuable hotels in the world . . . I will always be irritated . . . with myself.

A British woman wrote her memoirs of World War II, making reference to a short affair with a high-ranking British cabinet member. The publisher agreed to send the book's galleys to the aging politician to authenticate meetings and dates. The woman grew apprehensive that the man would be indignant because she had revealed their clandestine, extramarital liaison. A week later, she received a bouquet of long-stemmed roses and a note from him, which said, "I enjoyed reading about our time together during the Great Conflict. But when redoing the chapter about me and, in specific, our love making, must you make me sound so hurried?"

Most of life is finding the right pace.

NONVERBAL
COMMUNICATION

Sometimes stealth can become a valuable collaborator in negotiations. When I bring an ally (client, associate, or another participant) into the room, the secret communication between the ally and me can provide an edge during negotiations. Gestures, often unnoticed, provide the modus operandi for clandestine communication. To effect the secret message requires perfected and sometimes rehearsed nonverbal understanding between the two communicants. But in court with a witness on the stand, it would be foolish and improper for me to attempt these subtle gestures.

The most egregious gesture incident case occurred in the British television version of *Who Wants to Be a Millionaire?* A cheating conspiracy was alleged among a contestant, his wife, and a friend when video replays demonstrated a preplanned coughing sound that signaled the right answers.

I try to keep the gestures as few and easy as possible. If I touch my nose, the client knows beforehand to say "no." "No" is simple, but "yes" is more complex—a natural rubbing of an eye or a pull of the ear lobe.

It is commonplace for a client to forget the signals in the height of frenzied settlement negotiation. When this occurs, I jerk or pull my nose, rub my eye, and tug my ear. In truth, to everyone on the room, I must look like somebody who has Saint Vitus' dance or suffers from a horrible facial *douloureux tic.*

Some lawyers signal by kicking clients under the table. The problem is that it is easy to see a person kicking someone else in a small room. A second trouble arises when the surprised client reacts in pained shock from the sudden and unexpected shot to the shin. More glaring is a missed kick, especially if lawyers doing the leg jabbing slip lower and lower in their chairs until they have almost slid out of sight under the table. Such an obvious maneuver will not succeed.

Other attorneys blink eyes in code. One blink means "yes"; two blinks, "no." These eye movements parallel how a stroke victim answers questions. I tried this system once with horrible results. A client must be glued to the face of a lawyer to see and count accurately. Again, if the first blinking attempt is unseen, the attorney has to continue to blink away, looking like an idiot who cannot remove a cinder from an eyeball.

The eye rub was the best signal I could invent for "yes." I felt that the eye would stand for "aye," which would make some kind of sense to the person with whom I was trying to communicate. Over the years, I have tried, without success, to refine the "yes" and "no" signals by conceiving distinct facial expressions that could replace the touching. One attorney I knew could wiggle her ears, which she used like a semaphore.

GESTURE OF GOODWILL

Years ago, a man named Malcolm Horowitz owned a chain of juice stands in two cities where customers paid in cash. Mrs. Horowitz hired us as her fourth law firm in a divorce proceeding. The previous lawyers must have inquired about the considerable cash receipts that the juice business generated daily. But Horowtiz was evasive and the other attorneys did not pursue the cash trail.

When I interviewed the wife, she told me where the husband banked. I called the bank's safe-deposit department and learned that Horowitz had a safe-deposit box account in that branch. A safe-deposit box that is not indicated during the discovery process in a divorce usually suggests misdeeds.

I went to court alone, or ex parte (without notifying the other side), to see the judge handling the case. I asked for a signed order to open the safe-deposit box in the presence of the opposing lawyer and a bank officer. I had to seek relief ex parte because I realized that if the other side knew my intent, the husband would remove any money in the box before we had a chance to notify the bank of the court order. The judge permitted the search but told me that it would be futile since the case had reached its second year. In his opinion, even if the husband had once concealed cash in the safe-deposit box, he would have long since removed the monies.

I had nothing to lose and pushed for the judge to sign the order allowing me to serve the bank. After obtaining it, I could thereby seal the box until an inventory of its contents could be made. I contacted my adversary, who told me I was wasting everyone's time. He had spoken at length to Horowitz on the subject of cash a year earlier and his client assured him there were no hidden cash receipts in that safe-deposit box.

The day came to open the vault and box. Inside, it was stuffed with wads upon thick wads of cash, an astounding amount in small bills. The box was stuffed with so many bills that the bank had to obtain an electronic counter from another branch. Even with the electronic counter feeding bills into this machine at a rapid industrial conveyer belt rate, it required 90 minutes to arrive at a final tally of $1,100,000!

The husband had lied to his lawyer. Often a lawyer, like a cuckolded spouse, is the last to know.

We had discovered the hidden cache, the smoking gun of unreported income. At first reckoning, it seemed we had the husband trapped in a corner. He had understated the amount of assets in the marital pie, and he also faced the wrath of the Internal Revenue Service.

But I knew from experience that to allow the wife to coerce a settlement would doom her to a forever case. I knew what to expect: First, the husband would clear out the safe-deposit box after the contents had been inventoried. Next, he would file an amended tax return, reflecting the unreported amount. Then, he would pursue the divorce case to avoid having an uncontested record of charged illegal activities.

On occasion, the discovery of hidden cash creates a potential blackmail situation in the mind of the spouse. But if a spouse wants to go this underhanded route, they should hire a professional blackmailer and not my services as a lawyer and an officer of the court.

I said to the other attorney: "I am aware of the situation that may exist because of this unreported cash." This conversation, although not extortive in any way, was a professional communication by one lawyer telling the other of future intent. Indeed, we did not want to be involved in any fraud on the divorce court by concealing aspects of the financial picture. It sufficed that Horowitz's lawyer started thinking about the possible consequences for his client.

Since Horowitz's attorney and I were now familiar with the monies that would be left in the pot to divide, we acted as though the newly discovered money had been revealed all the time. The husband leaped at the chance to redress the clandestine and illegal deceit. It would be an expensive way out of his dilemma for him to pay half in taxes, interest, and penalties. But he would not dine on jailhouse food and serve time for criminal evasion of taxable income. I had given him a dignified and legal way out, a gesture that expedited the case and increased my client's share.

THE PAPER TRAIL

In law today, much litigation is conducted using the written word as opposed to the spoken. Papers are filed with the judge and then counterpapers are filed. Sometimes motions for temporary support (requests for awards based on papers) are granted, whereas other motions (paper filings) are aimed at the pleadings and technical aspects of the case.

I abhor lawyers who submit outrageous quantities of papers. They derive a false sense of power by dictating and dictating to a secretary; no matter what they say, no one answers back. No one says, "Cease!" They gaze with admiration at the pages and pages of words, which they see as utterances forever transcribed for posterity.

Often these lawyers submit papers to obscure their insecurity. The written pages mask the lack of guts to make statements in person. It is the Cyrano syndrome of hiding behind the bushes to avoid discovery. When I receive folios of offensive papers, I begin my legal reply in papers, "I do not choose to address the *ad hominem* (to the person or personal) comments in these papers."

My snub frustrates the lawyer-writer. The result is a second onslaught of more papers. The benefit to my client and me is that judges realize that by not responding, I am sending a subtle message to the court that these papers are without merit. The irony is that I make my point by doing nothing, which matches the nothing that my opponent has been doing with the endless papers.

SHORT PEOPLE WITH SHORTCOMINGS

I have observed that egocentric lawyers with unrelenting pesky behavior often are short men. I say this without rancor but as an anecdotal fact. I share this viewpoint with the designer Karl Lagerfeld, who said, "Women can be short, but for men it is impossible. . . . It is something that they will not forgive in life—to be born short."

I tried a custody case against Peter Bronstein, a skilled and well-known lawyer (height: about 5 feet 8 inches) in New York City who had just lost another case against me in a different county. In a colloquy with the judge, a frustrated Bronstein lost his temper and referred to me in court as "Fatty." (To be fair, at that time, I had gained a few extra pounds.) I retorted, "Mr. Bronstein, I could lose weight next month, but you cannot grow an inch taller." The judge broke up laughing and said, "He got you there, Mr. Bronstein." Bronstein remains a friend to this day.

I tried another case in a hearing where the option was to sit or stand, a decision that varies with the predilections of the referee. Once inside the proceeding, the referee chose informality and allowed the lawyers to sit at the same table. My adversary was an obnoxious, short lawyer. He finished a vicious tirade against me while standing. I said, "Judge, I could not tell if my opponent was sitting or standing during his presentation. So, I am going to opt on the side of the angels and stand during my turn." The remark was said innocently enough but my pocket-sized opponent became so furious that he could not perform during the rest of the case.

PHYSICAL DEFECTS

In my experience, dealing with people who have physical deformities is often difficult. Bernard Selklow, a lawyer in New York, was bright and articulate, but he was an angry man. He had a handicap: a withered arm (like Stalin and Kaiser William II) that gave him a certain animus toward life. I went out of my way to avoid dealing with him because there was no point in becoming involved in his ranting and diatribes.

An event after his death resulted in posthumous humiliation. He had had a romance late in life with a well-respected female lawyer in New York City. It was easy to understand how she had been attracted to him because he was a charismatic and forceful man. After he died, the woman tried to honor his memory by forming an association in his name, and she solicited donations from his friends and associates. But Selklow's family (ex-wife and children) took out an ad in the *New York Law Journal*, a publication read by most of the lawyers in the city, publicly disassociating themselves from the woman and her memorial efforts. It served to remind the legal community what a nasty person Selklow was: Even after his death, the family did not want to memorialize him. Or—in negative terms—maybe they did.

JUDGES AS DECIDERS

A court of equity will decide the division of assets in a divorce case. As in custody cases, equity is a carryover from English law when a chancellor, instead of a jury, determined the case. A historic maxim from English law states, "Justice varies as does the size of the chancellor's foot." Translation: On the same set of facts, the decision could vary, depending on which chancellor heard the case. The one-person method of deciding cases continues to the present day, and it is one of the most important reasons not to attack a judge with harsh words.

One of the sadder aspects of the American judicial system is that the everyday dispensing of justice varies from courtroom to courtroom. This is more evident in the federal judicial system than in the state courts. Each judge operates his own realm, enfeoffed to administer justice by the city, state, or federal authority. Judges are kings of their kingdom.

The proclivities of judges change from venue to venue and also the decorum and conduct of the courtroom vis-à-vis the attitudes of clerks, judges' secretaries, and judges' law assistants. If I come up against a nasty, belligerent, or indifferent judge, I will also experience nasty, belligerent, or indifferent law assistants and court personnel.

In 2003, a Supreme Court judge in Brooklyn received a jail sentence, and another one has been indicted. Divorce court cases in this segment of the court system located in the borough of Brooklyn operated as a criminal enterprise involving the judge, law guardian, and lawyers in payoffs. The odd part was that the judge involved, Gerald Garson, always behaved with perfect decorum every time I appeared before him. In fact, in one case where I represented the husband, he told me, *sua sponte* (by his own motion), he would have to remove himself from the case because he was related to the wife. The opposing counsel and his client knew that the wife was related to the judge, but they never told me. It was Judge Garson who did.

FINAL WORDS

I read a recent article about a new rule in China that requires judges to don black robes and to use a gavel in the courtroom. Why? Because in Western cultures, the black robe is an acknowledged symbol of the judge's authority, the silent message that the judge is in charge. A robed judge entering a courtroom achieves immediate credibility, and everyone in attendance stands as an act of respect.

The black robe sets the judge apart from the defense or prosecution, who are dressed in business suits or other professional attire. We see the judge as an impartial representative of the state whose credibility is not to be questioned or challenged.

9

VERBAL
COMMUNICATION

The two most important words in negotiations are *flexible* and *reasonable*. I promise that the resolution will proceed smoothly and more amicably if you insert those words into your opening statement. When someone states, "I know you are a reasonable and flexible person," it indicates your adversary is offering a pathway to an evenhanded negotiation. Implicit in the statement is that the customary conventions of comity and fairness will preside over the process.

As negotiations go forward, saying, "I assume you are reasonably flexible," in answer to any last offer can help move you closer to the desired result. Or you can state, "I have to think about this proposal, but I assume you will be reasonably flexible." This "reasonable-flexible" statement locks the other person into an intricate position of understood fairness.

No one wants to appear unreasonable or inflexible in a negotiation, or in any of life's matters. To be reasonably flexible is a positive attribute, and when you state your belief in plain words, the other party accepts it as a compliment. Conversely, you will find that few people claim, "I am not reasonably flexible," a negative trait that would undermine any negotiation process.

Fair-minded discussions reduce the number of damaging variables that can surface in any negotiation. Being flexible and reasonable prevents the negotiation from turning uncomplicated matters into complex ones. Once an opponent and I find an avenue to a solution, we then move straight toward settlement. A harmonious end is possible if both sides stay within the parameters of "flexible and reasonable."

WORDS FOR JUDGES

Sophocles wrote, "How dreadful it is when the right judge judges wrong!" My task is to try to steer judges to rule more favorably for my client or, at minimum, to listen to a new line of argument. Yet, I have to be very careful in my approach to judges and cautious about the words I choose.

A judge is similar to an adversary except that a judge starts in a neutral position, whereas adversaries are always on the other side of the fence. Of course, neutral judges become my adversaries when they side with the opposition. I can walk away from a negotiation with an adversary, but it is impossible to walk away from a judge. Aggressive behavior will fail with a judge, as will about half of the other clever negotiation ploys that I use against opponents.

I never meet judges head-on with a battering ram, nor do I create an impasse by forcing judges into a tight spot from which they cannot find an easy way out. No productive negotiation will occur if the opening verbal salvo is negative and destructive to the judge, spouse, or an associate.

A diplomatic tactic I use with judges is to say, "Your honor, I know you are trying to be fair, but I do not believe your analysis is fair to my client." Notice that I have used the word "fair," which is what a judge is hired to be. Praising a judge for being fair is an appreciative comment. I anticipate that the judge will accept the tribute and then perhaps revisit a position.

The "please be fair" speech also reiterates to the judge that impartiality is what both sides expect. After I open with this entreaty, I quote the law and precedence to back up my contention that my client is being treated unfairly. My objective is to widen the parameters of the judge's thinking. Judges listen to this rational argument because I have not insulted their rulings or their intelligence.

In one case, the adversary lawyer and I met with the judge in her chambers. I was unhappy that the judge had ruled against me and I said to her, "Your honor, you were correct on 96.5 percent in this ruling." The odd statement startled the judge. In her mind, it must have registered, "Hey, that's a pretty good score. Felder thinks I am 96.5 percent correct. Maybe, to score a 100 percent, I should listen to the other 3.5 percent of his argument." And she did. The statement allowed me to find the opening to drive home my point.

A technique I use with hostile judges is to ask in a good-humored fashion: "Your honor, why are you beating up on me? My client has a position. Maybe you do not agree with 75 percent of it. But, please, keep an open mind. I am just doing my job and you have no good reason to punish the messenger." Most judges understand that when a lawyer expresses these feelings, it is a subjective conclusion. Judges do not want a lawyer to walk away thinking that the court's actions were unfair or, worse that they beat up on an attorney because of that lawyer's advocacy stance. Often, a judge will respond by saying, "Look, I am not beating up on you. I disagree, but . . ." and again it opens up the negotiation for more give-and-take.

On rare occasions—emphasis on the "rare"—if the judge rules against a client, it may be in the interests of the lawyer to make the judge angry. The aim is to have a higher court reverse the ruling on appeal. Occasionally when lawyers hit a raw nerve, provoked judges may make intemperate remarks in anger. If they rule in an atypical way, it might create a favorable review by an appellate court and a determination of reversible error. Or the appellate court could find that the judge overreached and then reverse the decision unfavorable to my client. This represents a last desperate maneuver—the near impossible "Hail Mary" pass with time running out.

A Judge-Baiting Incident

New business establishments often have names derived from the first or last names of the partners. Two of the nation's largest companies exemplify this practice: Mattel (from Harold *Mat*son and *Eliot* Handler) and Revlon (originally "Revlach,") derived from *Rev*son and Charles *Lach*man. When it became the more elegant sounding Revlon, the "l" in the new company name was all that was left from Lachman's name.

Lachman, who was a chemist, perfected methods to produce nail polish and lipsticks in matching shades of color. The idea came from Revson, the company's salesman. Lachman was eased out of the company, exiting as a wealthy man. He divorced his wife and began a genteel retirement. Later he married a European woman and lived many months abroad while still maintaining U.S. citizenship.

Rita Lachman, the former wife, hired me to bring on a conservatorship proceeding. The object was to prove that Lachman had become senile and that the court should appoint a conservator of his estate. One fact we used was that Lachman and his new wife lived in the South of France and—*sacre bleu*—used the American flag as a doormat!

I hoped to prove that Lachman was helpless and unable to handle his own affairs. We braced for bad luck when the judge assigned in this case turned out to be in his mid-seventies, about the same age as Lachman. I would have a difficult time proving that age was the main contributor to the senility in front of another elderly person who presided over the dispute.

When trial court decisions come up for appeal, the appellate court sees a printed record of documents or items allowed into evidence. It does not see or hear the witnesses being examined, nor does it review the physical evidence. When I read the daily printed record of the Lachman conservatorship case, I realized it did not reflect the lack of sensitivity and even contempt the elderly judge had for my position. The record was "clean," as lawyers say. The judge in a cursory and indifferent manner had decided against my client. I had a losing case.

On the last day of hearings, the judge said he was going to decide from the bench. He asked the lawyers to make closing arguments after which he would render a verdict, having considered arguments and evidence. However, I spotted the judge's typed decision on his desk; he had already rejected the proposal for conservatorship. The summations he asked for would have no effect on a decision already written. The final speeches were cosmetic, to make it appear that each side presented their case in full and that he had considered fairly the arguments.

When it was my turn for summation, I said, "Judge, I see before you a decision. What's the point of asking me to sum up when you've already made up your mind?" The judge became angry, stood up, and threw the papers at the desk. Enraged, he threatened judicial review and personal censure. I had a created a possible scenario of an out-of-control judge whose irrational decision could be assailed on appeal.

Another case along these lines occurred when I represented a husband in a bitter child custody case with his nonworking wife. She had hired a large corporate firm to represent her interests. The trial judge was a married woman with three children. In the opposing counsel's summation, the lawyer blabbered on about the adverse effects seen in children whose mothers had full-time employment. This was the wrong tack to take with the full-time, working female judge. My client was awarded custody of the child based on other negative information about the wife, but my adversary's poor judgment did not help his client's case.

I tried a case involving the Satmar religious group. This fervent sect of Hasidic Judaism maintains insular communities where people wear special clothing, follow a strict schedule of prayer and religious study, and customarily, speak Yiddish at home. The sect does not recognize the state of Israel because it is a secular state and does not conform to the vision of the Holy Land as a religious home. The Satmars do not seem to have advanced from a mystical mind-set dating back to the Middle Ages.

I represented a woman who had been a member of the Rockland County Satmar group. She had married another Satmar and they had two children, but then she decided to break away from the community and divorce her husband, actions that angered the other sect members. They believed that leaving the sect and obtaining a divorce were acts of heresy.

At first, unable to escape from the group, she and her children boarded with another Satmar household. Life there was also hell. She reported that in the new living quarters, the husband, a father with five children, often sat on the stairs and ran his hand up her leg as she climbed up and down. He continued this sexual assault at the same time he was publicly condemning her. This behavior infuriated me; it was an infringement on my client's constitutional right to choose another, more secular life.

At trial, to demonstrate the destructive primitiveness of the sect, I described how my client's husband almost caused the death of one of their children. When the infant was seriously ill, the husband refused to call a local doctor for treatment. Instead, he journeyed miles and hours to Brooklyn to convince the rabbi there to return to Rockland County. When the rabbi arrived, he said a special prayer for wellness and left a charm in the crib. In the father's

mind, these hocus-pocus actions would be more effective in cur-
ing the child's illness than a visit by a physician.

In a custody case, the court does not let a jury decide, which
is a direct carryover from English law and the concept of courts of
equity. At the end of the trial in this case, I made an impassioned
plea to the judge. I pointed out the deprivations the woman had
suffered, the scorn and contempt heaped on her by the community, and the recklessness of the husband's actions in the marriage.
The judge ruled for my client.

But here's the twist: The appellate court overruled the judge's
decision! I was shocked. On what possible legal grounds could this
open-and-shut case have been reversed? The appellate court sent it
back for a new trial on a unique ground: It claimed my closing argument *inflamed* the judge! This is a ground for appellate reversal
when a summation might be considered to have inflamed a jury.
This case represented the sole instance in memory where a summation was held to have incensed the judge and caused a new trial.

In fact, this is one of the principal reasons a judge decides in
custody cases, and not a jury. Juries can become swayed by passion, whereas judges are trained to decide cases on facts and without emotion. The judge's decision in the case was correct.

The end to this story still causes me melancholy. I had devoted much time and effort on the custody case, taking it on pro
bono (without pay). But when the case was to be retried, I could
not afford to become further involved with this brave woman.
Later, I was told that rather than go to trial again, she ran off to
make a new life, disappearing with her children into the American
heartland.

Ultimatums Not

An egregious mistake people make is to allow their feelings to
erupt in a volcanic explosion. In negotiating, what you say will

express these feelings more explicitly than what you do. Often harmful language results. These angry outbursts, or ultimatums, often throw a wrench into the proceedings and should be avoided.

If you appear aggressive and choose antagonistic language, it will raise your opponents' hackles. The message you convey is "I am in charge of these procedures. I am giving orders. Do what I say." The tactic may work with a cowed spouse or with young children (followed by furious backtalk or future vows of disobedience), but the words are provocative and destructive to an amicable settlement.

The worst single word to use in negotiation is "no." Standing alone and without a qualifying explanation, the word no will torpedo any discussion and sink the prospects for settlement. It is important to leave an opponent a way out that will save face. A good negotiator always provides a reasonable position from which an adversary can walk away and return with a reasonable counteroffer.

Code Words

I learned the importance of code words and hidden signals from the late Milton "Mickey" Rudin, the preeminent entertainment lawyer. He represented Frank Sinatra, Elizabeth Taylor, Lucille Ball, and other A-List Hollywood celebrities during a long and distinguished career. The Harvard-trained attorney twice argued cases before the Supreme Court.

Rudin acted as Sinatra's attorney, business manager, pal, and confidant for 35 years. He felt that he was responsible for much of Sinatra's wealth by steering the singer into lucrative real estate investments. Rudin was convinced that when he died, his tombstone would read, "Here lies Frank Sinatra's lawyer."

Later in the relationship, Sinatra dumped Rudin, a spiteful act that was a persistent and unattractive part of the singer's complex character. He would develop close relationships with people and then violently rupture the attachment. He suddenly dropped Peter Lawford, one of the Rat Pack. He also discarded his first business manager, Hank Sanicola, and George Jackson, his valet of 15 years.

In the 1940s before he was known as "The Voice," Sinatra hired ace publicist George Evans, who had the genius idea to hire teenage girls—called bobby-soxers in the early 1940s—to scream and swoon at Sinatra's performance at the Paramount Theatre in New York City. Evans stationed ambulances outside the Paramount Theatre ready to take any bobby-soxers who fainted to nearby hospitals. Police had to restrain the tumultuous teenage crowds and those screeching Paramount performances marked the beginning of Sinatra's meteoric rise to fame. Soon afterward, he fired George Evans in a New York minute.

I first met Rudin in the 1980s as an adversary. We became friendly, and then he began referring cases to me. He related that Sinatra did not like to refuse people who asked him to perform at a particular charity function, or at an event where he would not be well paid. Sinatra would whisper to Rudin, "GMO." GMO meant "Get Me Out." Rudin played the bad guy, while Sinatra could always play the good guy in response to these requests. He also used Lee Salters, his long-time press agent, in the same way. Later in life, however, when he was at the top of his career, Sinatra was generous with his time at fund-raisers and charitable events.

In the early 1950s, Sinatra fell into the abyss of public indifference after changes in the public's taste for music. A little known fact is that he signed a deal with Capital Records in 1952 for the boilerplate minimum. He then appeared in *From Here to Eternity*, which marked the beginning of one of the most brilliant second acts in the history of U.S. performing arts. He reached the pinnacle of stardom becoming almost a deified, mythical figure. It was as if people ascribed miraculous powers to the touch of his hand.

Sinatra always was surrounded by people to advise him in various aspects of life—everything from performing, to appearing at political events and making the right investments. Like many eminent people, he did not take advice kindly, although he did listen. Part of the problem was that he was not well educated and resented the "suits" (lawyers, accountants, businesspeople) talking down to him. He turned against anyone who *told* him what to do.

Sinatra's motto was, "Suggest. Don't tell." He favored people who asked him questions like, "Frank, what would you *think* about appearing on Jerry Lewis's Muscular Dystrophy Telethon?" He would ignore an associate who said, "Frank, you *should* do the telethon with Jerry."

Sinatra had some peculiar quirks; he was often dismissive and insulting to people who worked for him, writing off old friends. Yet, he could turn down performing at a venue for a large sum of money and instead attend a party where he would sing for two hours. Often after he finished his last show, he would visit local hospitals with the request that the performance not be publicized.

I represented the Damon Runyon estate, and at one time Sinatra wanted to do a movie based on the famous writer's career, in which he would play the larger-than-life Runyon. He had already appeared as Nathan Detroit in the movie *Guys and Dolls*. When we met, I found Sinatra rather ordinary looking, hardly the matinee idol that I had imagined conquering all those Hollywood beauties. His famous blue eyes, juxtaposed against a darker complexion, were his only striking feature. His voice had the modulated tones of a radio announcer, but his language and accent were New York or, more precisely, New Jersey.

In the same way that Sinatra's associates learned to approach him, I have learned it is helpful not to tell people what to do, but to suggest. In a social situation at home, I might say, for example, "What do you think about taking the children to Moose Head Lake for the summer?" If this has been an area of dispute, it suggests a possibility instead of demanding approval. I implant the suggestion by asking for a response.

REPRESENTATION

To represent a person, I have to believe I am on the right side of the issue, and I have to accept as true that what I am urging also has merit. I must believe in my cause before I can convince another.

I can always spot people who are disingenuous, particularly, when matters become heated. They lose the passion for the fight because they do not believe in the merit of their argument.

Years ago, the U.S. Navy did an interesting double-blind medical study. It picked two groups of patients, both suffering from diabetes. It handed two sets of doctors a harmless placebo, but told one group that it had received a revolutionary new drug. The other group was told it was a placebo and received instructions to lie to their patients about this new "wonder drug" cure. Both sets of doctors told their patients, "Here is a new miracle drug for diabetes." The result? The patients that received the placebo from the doctors who believed it was a miracle drug had a marginally higher recovery rate than those taking the placebo from the doctors who knew they were not dispensing a miracle cure. The mind has the power to heal the body.

A mysterious authenticity or telecommunication passes from a speaker who believes to the person who hears the message, whether it is in medicine, law, or life.

NEGATIVE APPROACHES

Sometimes an adversary confronts me and says, "Felder, I am not afraid of your reputation. I am going to knock your socks off in this divorce case. Don't try to pull those tired old tricks with me." I know from experience that this lawyer has an agenda other than settling the case, which is the one objective that is in the client's best interest.

Typically, verbal challenges at the beginning of a negotiation are superfluous bluster originating from unsuccessful or youthful attorneys. The former are people filled with anger at their own lack of success in the law and in life. The latter are the wannabe Hotspurs looking to make a fast reputation by taking on their more famous seniors. In either scenario, the results are unproductive.

The best strategy with these blowhards and egotistical gasbags is let them talk and talk until the last breaths of hot air and venom have dribbled out of their mouths. Once a hostile opponent has fired off all the rounds from his clip, he is done for. I answer by saying calmly, "I do not think that this is a good time to start negotiations. When you put the animus aside and want to begin meaningful discussions, we'll reschedule." End of diatribe, end of meeting.

By not engaging my opponent in counterattack, I leave room in the process for the presentation of facts. Good lawyers realize that negotiations will continue based on the merits of the case. Rules of reason and precedence will apply. A personal vendetta will not produce a good resolution. The injured party will be the client of the frothing-at-the-mouth lawyer.

LISTENING

An adversary's vocabulary is more important than your own. By listening to the opening choice of words, you will learn two important facts: whether the tone of the negotiations will be reasonable or adversarial, and the pattern of the scripted speech. In the negotiation opera, the tone becomes the music and the pattern provides the lyrics.

Two types of people make unsuccessful negotiators: those who are in love with what they say, and those who are in love with the sound of what they say. Marcel Proust said that what you love is not important; it is being in love that is important. If I am in the company of a loquacious person who loves to listen to the sound of his own voice, my strategy is to let him ramble on. Soon, his positions will dissolve into the air or self-destruct because he has talked them to death. Most people have a limited repertoire and when I let them play their music, the song is soon over.

Sherlock Holmes said to Watson, "You hear but you don't listen." By listening, you project the image of a reasonable person. Listening says you are open to learning the facts. Listening says that you are open to negotiation, want to hear new thoughts, and respect the other person. Listening allows both sides to progress along a parallel track to settlement.

Key to listening is to identify what part of your opponent's argument is the most important. Often, attorneys will repeat or emphasize the main thrust of the argument. Think of it as the theme returning again and again like the violin music weaving through Rimsky-Korsakov's *Scheherazade*.

I took part in a mediation before Judge Milton Mollen, a distinguished New York figure in the judiciary. After retiring from the bench, his services were available as a private mediator in disputes. At our initial appearance, Judge Mollen asked each side to make a brief presentation of their client's position, explaining what we deemed were the significant aspects of the matter at hand. My adversary began, "I am owed $375,000," and then followed with his views about the case. I saw Judge Mollen's silent, disapproving reaction when the lawyer mentioned his unpaid fee as the case's most important point. The epilogue was that it was one of the few cases that this learned judge was unsuccessful in mediating. My adversary proved so unreasonable that the case went to court, where he lost—and his client lost out on millions of dollars.

Talking Too Much

Newspaper reporters told me the story about a well-known lawyer who had a winning case, representing a public figure in a criminal case. At the summation, he talked and talked and talked, and his big mouth talked his client into a conviction. As Winston Churchill said of Clement Atlee, "He had the ability to snatch defeat from the jaws of victory."

When I know that I have a joint meeting with my client and my adversary is a compulsive chatterbox, I make it a point to inform my client ahead of time that I am going to listen without responding to my opponent. Otherwise, my client will sit in the room and grow agitated that I do not make counterjabs at the other attorney's loquacious attack.

I studied medicine before law and still remember the advice of a wise physician, "Listen, and the patient will tell you what is wrong with him." I tell young lawyers that if they listen to clients and to the other party's presentation, the case—with its problems, strengths, and weaknesses—will become clear.

Name-Calling

Threatening or offensive language will put a spike in the negotiations with serious, if not fatal, consequences. When you call opponents vile names, they will retaliate with name-calling of their own or become so offended that they will act unreasonably and not want to continue to settlement.

A calamitous negotiation occurred in 1966 when the New York City Transit Workers Union (TWU) went out on strike for two weeks during the first term of Mayor John Lindsey (who was the city's best looking and least effective mayor). Some historians believe that it was an accident waiting to happen when the patrician and overconfident Lindsey underestimated (and some said, insulted) Michael J. Quill, the working-class boss of the TWU.

No sooner had Lindsey been elected in November 1965, when the TWU issued its usual demands to renew the expiring contract, asking for higher wages and a reduced workweek. Unlike his predecessor, Mayor Robert Wagner, Lindsey did not participate in the negotiations, delegating the transactions to subordinates. At the same time, the Lindsey crowd assailed the anachronistic Quill in the press, vilifying him as "an irresponsible demagogue." Worse, they enjoyed calling him a "lawless hooligan," a direct reference to the word's eponymous origin from Patrick Hooligan, a noted nineteenth-century Irish hoodlum.

All the disparate elements came together like a runaway train, and on the morning of January 1, 1966, subways and buses stopped running. The TWU had gone on strike. The great metropolis would witness 10 days of hardship before another bus or subway moved in the city.

This affair reveals the classic do's and don'ts of negotiation. First, the vicious name-calling by the Lindseyites against Quill stiffened the union boss's back. The verbal attacks also rallied the union's rank and file who perceived that their standard-bearer's name was being dragged in the mud. Second, Lindsey's failure to adhere to mayoral precedence and participate face-to-face in the negotiating process was a nonverbal communication that he was disinterested in the process and believed negotiating with Quill was beneath him. Lindsey, in fact, had vacationed in Puerto Rico after the November election, which the union took as a haughty affront. Third, and most important, as the deadline passed, the TWU did carry out a strike, its one weapon. Lindsey had underestimated his adversary with disastrous results. Quill had threatened a walkout and, when negotiations broke down, he carried through on that promise, even though he went to jail.

Perhaps Quill, who died a few weeks after the settlement, enjoyed the last laugh. Few recall today the barrage of negative remarks the media and Lindsey's people voiced against the union leader. But a few older New Yorkers can still remember Quill's thick Irish brogue, purposely mispronouncing or, more accurately, cheerily slurring the Mayor's name as "Linsley."

Lindsey, on the other hand, suffered an almost unimaginable, heartrending last chapter in his life. I represented the National Arts Club and saw him at one of their dinners a few months before his death. He was physically shrunken and wore an ill-fitting, tattered tuxedo. Unfortunately, his matinee-idol, movie star good looks had dissipated. He had fallen on bad times financially and could not even afford health insurance. Mayor Rudolph Giuliani came to Lindsey's rescue and promulgated a private bill that provided him with health insurance in his final days.

BAD WORDS, GOOD CLIENTS

A little knowledge of the law is a dangerous thing. Clients acquire a casual concept of the law from watching *Court TV,* reading the legal thrillers of John Grisham or Scott Turow, or speaking with a friend who has been involved in litigation. Often, clients will suggest a strategy that goes something like this: "I was speaking to my friend Marcy who was divorced last year after receiving a large settlement. Marcy's divorce attorney destroyed her husband, taking his possessions and putting him penniless out on the street. Let's do that."

In front of an attorney, clients may have so little ego that they are afraid to say, "I had this idea." Instead, they disguise thoughts by saying, "I have spoken to a number of people who think . . ." Or, "I have a friend whose husband is a lawyer and he believes that . . ." A lawyer's job is to understand where these remarks are coming from and treat the comments with respect. I have found that it is the clients' own lack of self-worth that makes them put forward such ideas to the lawyer.

Clients may speak to someone whose opinion they think their own lawyer would respect. When they relate the conversation, they filter it through the prism of what they believe produced a winning past outcome. The truth is that lawyers listen to what clients say and try to keep an open mind even when another person's opinion is dropped into the talks. But most lawyers I know listen with a jaundiced ear.

After clients tell me their friend's advice, instead of becoming angry, I show appreciation for the suggestion. I say, "That is an interesting approach, and I thank you for bringing it to me. But it is not relevant in our case." If the client supplies enough details, I may be able to demonstrate the differences in the references.

Or, if clients suggest a course of action with a request for me to investigate, I wait until the next session and use a third party's voice. I say, "My associate looked into that legal question you posed, and she does not think it will work in our negotiation."

I was the lawyer for a jittery woman in an estate case. Her questions were like a staccato interrogation. She took exhaustive notes on a legal pad and insisted on knowing details, including precedence cases. Her nephew was a first-year law student at Cornell University, and she reviewed the case with him on a daily basis. Then, at our next meeting, she would say, " Sonny thinks that it might be better if we filed so-and-so motion."

I endured this harmless kibitzing for a few sessions. Then, at the most significant moment in the case, I said, "It's critical that we file this motion today. Or, if you like, we can wait for Sonny's opinion." And I said this with as much sincerity as I could muster. She never brought up her nephew's name again.

Another way to stifle anonymous third-party interference is to say to the client: "Look, I have to speak with Mr. Smith [the source of the comments], with whom you've been talking; I am uneasy about proceeding because he may have a very good idea. It could be that I am off base on the next course of action so I do not want to proceed without his opinion." Indeed, I could end the invisible third-person problem by saying, "I refuse to listen to any further advice unless the person is interested enough to sit and discuss it with me. I am prepared to listen to the other person's ideas." The client will never ever let you meet "Mr. Smith" even if the person exists, and most of the time he does not. And if Mr. Smith exists, he has given the advice with a caveat that he does not want to become involved. The third party never wants to play the difficult hand, just to comment invisibly from the sidelines.

A problem in the legal profession is that the vocabulary of law is the same as the vocabulary of everyday conversation. Lawyers employ Latin terms like *nunc pro tunc, duces tecum, in terrorem,*, and *pro haec vice.* However, aside from a small Latin vocabulary, we do not employ an esoteric or unique language as do doctors or engineers.

Lawyers speak the same language as the client.

The client does not appreciate that the language of law is a form of professional communication. This creates an extra burden on the lawyer who must relate the case in everyday speech, often conveying complicated legal concepts and arguments. The client interprets the ordinary language of the law as meaning, "I am as smart as my lawyer. He uses the same words that I use."

Foul Language

In the beginning of my career when I worked for the Department of Justice, I would salt my remarks with an occasional four-letter word when dealing with colleagues and adversaries. In the milieu of criminal law, a solitary curse did not merit a second thought. In the more civilized arena of divorce (an arguable proposition), cursing in front of clients or opposing counsel sends a harmful message unless you use it judiciously.

Cursing, by a person unskilled in the art, is a form of noncommunication and antilanguage, just as rap is a form of antimusic. Both, however, can convey a sense of outrage. Cursing interrupts communication. It serves no purpose other than as a distraction that some lawyers use for camouflage when unprepared.

In a few past cases, opposing attorneys cursed me in front of their clients to demonstrate the tough approach they were prepared to take. The lawyer would sometimes call later to apologize, citing the theatrical need to demonstrate belligerence in front of a client. Usually, the lack of culture that impels this form of human communication precludes an apology.

On one occasion, I was negotiating with a firm whose lead counsel was notorious for his nasty vocabulary. My female client sought resolution, and at the meeting the foul-mouthed lawyer sat in with a female associate from his firm. No sooner had we presented a reasonable array of offers, than the room was filled with a prolific broadside of his profanity. When the female associate tried to calm her senior partner down, he shouted at her with a sailor's tongue. My client and I left the room at once. Later that afternoon, the female associate called to say that her firm had agreed to our demands. She was mortified at the partner's behavior and apologized. On a confidential basis, she said, "I never again want to fall into that man's mouth." As I later discovered, a more accurate reason for the success of our position was that the foul-mouth's own client said he would not tolerate cursing in front of his wife. He also threatened to hire another lawyer if it happened again.

Expanding Women's Rights

Beginning in the 1960s and culminating in the 1980s, divorce in the United States became more or less "decriminalized" (for want of a better word). Fault in New York went out the window in 1967.

Prior to July 19, 1980, adultery was the sole grounds for divorce in New York state. Equitable distribution also took effect in 1987 and it has been the good rule ever since.

In addition to the general tendency for no-fault or decriminalized divorce, the division of assets also evolved. Legislators of various states approached divorce as a breakdown similar to the breakup of a business partnership. When partners dissolve a business, the assets are divided and who might have been more to blame for the failure does not determine whether one party receives a larger percentage than another. States regarded divorce as the splitting up of a union, much of it financial. The husband's contribution was obvious because he worked and made the money. The at-home wife's and mother's participation was an important nonfinancial contribution. The division held up when the genders were reversed, which has happened on frequent occasions these past three decades.

The available marital pot increased substantially after divorce became decriminalized and laws were enacted dividing the parties' assets under the theory of equitable distribution or communal property. These changes witnessed the expansion of rights of wives as new divorce issues relating to asset allocation came before the appellate courts.

The rights of wives broadened as women formed groups and then centralized their concerns to legislators ultimately forming a powerful voting block. Legislators who did not listen to these voices of change were voted out of office. Organized women's groups on local, state, and federal levels sent out thousands of pieces of literature, and formed political action groups to push their messages across.

Men were never so organized. If a man obtains an unsatisfactory result in a divorce case, chances are he will be found complaining to a bartender. A woman, on the other hand, who does not like the result of the case will meet with other women, form an advocacy group, or join one—and try to change the law.

Judges of both genders were not happy about the mounting pressure from these women's groups, especially the ones that monitored the court system. Judges were now under scrutiny when spectators from the women's organizations viewed and recorded the actions and activities in the courtroom.

We tried a case in Suffolk County, New York. The trial had already begun when a female member of one of these advocacy groups, attempted to speak to the judge in his chambers after court. The judge met with the woman, responded cordially, and asked the reason for the colloquy. She blurted out her observations and concerns about the case and the mortified judge had to declare a mistrial. All the time, money, and emotional effort that had been spent were now wasted, and the case had to start over from scratch.

In the judicial system, it may be dangerous for special groups to try to affect the legislature. I am a staunch advocate for animal rights supporters who have accomplished the passing of laws on the care and treatment of animals. But divorce law is not so defined in black and white. In divorce, one finds a broad-reaching societal effect that seeks a judicial rearranging of the economy by a redistribution of the wealth.

The rights of women increase each time the law is reviewed. For example, it makes sense to give a wife a portion of, or to divide up, a pension fund that has been accumulated during the marriage. But the question is: Does it make sense to put a monetary value on a professional career or practice? The courts will put a value on that practice after listening to expert testimonies. These values are smoke and mirrors unrelated to the real world. Most careers or professional practices cannot be given away, borrowed against, hypothecated, or sold as a bona fide asset. Yet the husband may have to pay 50 percent of the arrived-at, calculated value of the practice in a divorce settlement.

I do not say that wives should be deprived of some financial gain and recognition in this area. But the question of basic fairness must be addressed when money is awarded and disbursed based on a future that may not exist. An example would be opera singers who are sued for divorce, with a value fixed on their current and future celebrity. In the real world, opera singers' fame is unlikely to lead to requests for product endorsements, or what happens if they develop a throat condition and retire from the stage? Or, what about doctors just graduated from medical school? How to put a price on their future earnings when they may choose to join the armed services or do altruistic work for little compensation?

Is it fair to put a value on a plastic surgeon's entire practice when most patients who come for treatment want to see a particular partner—and that surgeon generates the most income? If the surgeon dies, is the practice then worth anything? In today's divorce system, an enormous value is placed on the practice with no consideration given for life's contingencies.

Seeing Double

I tried a case once where a Catholic priest was having an affair with my client's wife. Pictures were taken of the priest in civilian clothes entering a motel with the woman. The priest had a twin brother who came to court, pretending that he had been the person in the photograph and that it was he who had been intimate with the wife. My client, the jury, and even the judge believed in their mind and hearts that the adulterer was the priest, whose reputation was being saved by an altruistic act like that of Sydney Carton in *A Tale of Two Cities*. But my client, a practicing Catholic, did not want to put the priest in such a compromising position and was happy to have the divorce taken against him. My assumption was that wife, husband, priest, jury, and judge were all happy to sweep the repugnant tale under the carpet.

Forty years ago, a character named Tommy Manville floated in New York cafe society. He was the wealthy heir to the Johns-Manville Company asbestos fortune (this was years before the company went belly-up after paying out millions for asbestos illnesses). When I knew him, he was an aging playboy, a roué, and rich. On meeting a pretty girl, his first words were typically, "Will you marry me?" He had 12 or 13 wives and one memorable divorce quote: "She cried, and the judge wiped her tears with my checkbook."

A woman visited my office to say that Manville (then deceased) had married her, and then they divorced in Las Vegas. She swore, however, that on the day of the divorce she was not feeling well and asked her look-alike sister to stand in court before the judge. She declared that the divorce was null and void and she remained the playboy's lawful widow, now pressing a claim to his vast estate. A fortune in today's money rested on which twin had the Toni. The story was reported in the press. The woman's story did not impress me, and she lost the case later with another attorney.

CLIENT ATTACKS

Some women request that I "go after" their husbands in the conferences. The problem is if I say to the husband, "You're a despicable SOB," the husband and his attorney respond with, "Raoul, you're a bigger SOB and, if you hate us, we hate you double." Where does this verbal assault lead? Nowhere.

On occasion, I will make fun of the husband's girlfriend. This tactic brings the paramour into the room in a provocative manner, but not in a way that poisons the air and removes the possibility of realistic negotiations. At a meeting, I may ask an innocent yet embarrassing question about the other woman and then watch the husband squirm in his seat. I have no interest in the vengeance value, but making the man uncomfortable opens the door to negotiate a better deal for my client.

I might use a ploy of discussing finances to introduce the other woman. In following the money and business trail, I begin questioning the husband about monies he has spent, reviewing past credit card statements. I may spot a rental car charge and ask, "When you rented this car, was it solely for your private use or did someone else share the benefit of the car rental?" I know that the husband drove somewhere with the girlfriend. Or if I see payment for a hotel room in a resort, a legitimate question is, "Was this room shared with any one else?" The other side will object. But I ask these questions to allocate back to the wife a percentage of the family monies that the paramour enjoyed. The goal is to increase the wife's asset pot and introduce the other woman without making a moral judgment.

Taking the Fifth

In some states even today, adultery remains a crime, and a witness is allowed to invoke the Fifth Amendment against self-incrimination. A jury in a criminal case is instructed that no inference can be given because someone has invoked the Fifth Amendment. In a civil case, however, the law permits a theory of fact that allows judge and jury to draw adverse inferences when someone "takes the Fifth." When a husband invokes his right against self-incrimination in a civil trail, I paint as broad a canvas of adultery as I can.

Taking the Fifth means embarking on a trip from which there is often no detour. When I have a witness who takes the Fifth in a civil case, I am secure in the knowledge that the witness will answer none of my questions. After a series of probing questions—all unanswered—I subtly paint a picture of events more sinister or hurtful than they really are.

In these situations, a husband may be inclined to opt for a more generous negotiated settlement to avoid going down a road that is embarrassing both to him and to his paramour.

FLATTERING WORDS

Flattery can generate allies in negotiations. The trick is not to overdo it, not to appear fawning or obsequious, and to know the limits of charm. If I overpraise a judge, it will do more harm than good to my case.

For some people, flattery is a kind of bright light that illuminates them like a Christmas tree. When I represented the wife of George Barrie, he told me an anecdote in the course of litigation. Barrie, the owner of Brut-Faberge, was a pioneer in signing up celebrities for his line of cosmetics, including 007's Roger Moore, Joe Namath, Muhammad Ali, and Cary Grant.

At first, Grant was reluctant to become a spokesperson, but Barrie persisted. Because he knew that the handsome actor enjoyed having people tell him how wonderful he was, Barrie took Grant on promotional junkets to cosmetics factories and arranged for the most adoring line workers—mostly older, blue-haired ladies—to line up and meet him. They would beg for autographs and shamelessly flatter the debonair star. Grant loved the adulation, beaming after each factory visit. He valued the admiration (all of it sincere) more than the money, which is saying a lot since Grant reputedly was a tightwad.

I had dealings with a well-known New York lawyer who was more show than substance. In fact, he knew little about the law or how to practice it. His ego was the size of Alaska, and he once bragged that a famous judge praised him as one of the best lawyers to appear before him. I was astounded because this attorney had the reputation of being a legal dolt. Several days later, I bumped into the judge and mentioned the lawyer's remark. The judge laughed and said, "That man was terrible in court. Before I gave him the bad news and told him he lost the case, I said: 'This is one of the most difficult custody cases I have ever seen and I must compliment the fine work. But the facts are such I was constrained to rule the other way.'" Everyone emerged a winner.

I once hired a lawyer who turned out to be a chronic nuisance to the office staff and me. I was not happy with her legal skills and decided to appoint her as the firm's managing attorney, which is not a high office. It is a clerical job to ensure that the other lawyers in the firm are aware of the deadlines for their cases and follow the legal calendars. A "managing attorney" should not be confused with a managing partner; the latter is the head of the firm. After this lawyer left my employ, I heard from different sources that she crowed to everyone that she had risen to the position of managing attorney in my firm. I cannot believe that she thought this perfunctory title was an impressive compliment, but maybe it had some sway on less sophisticated clients.

Many settlements are made before a jury trial begins. Judges, to some degree, assist in the resolution. Sometimes they help by doing and saying nothing, representing a wordless presence of authority. The silent judge evokes the image that justice will be administered if the two parties cannot work out a settlement. When a settlement is reached, I make a complimentary remark on the record concerning the judge's helpful input. I make this statement because it is true even in the most benign cases, and it also makes the judge feel good. Who knows if or when I shall meet this judge again?

NOMENCLATURE

Rudy Guiliani, the former mayor of New York, had to deal with the gigantic mixed population that is New York City. His task was difficult because he became mayor in an era of exacerbated racial and ethnic conflicts, coupled with emerging urban racial and ethnic pride.

Once when I visited the mayor at his City Hall office, I observed that several times even in private conversation with an aide, he used politically and socially acceptable terms to describe the large number of ethnic communities in the New York City. I was struck by the consideration the mayor and his administration demonstrated—both in public and private—when referring to the city's disparate groups in the acceptable terminology of their own choosing.

It may sound naïve but I always thought, for example, that the words "Hispanic" and "Latino" were interchangeable, referring to any American who came from a Spanish-speaking country. This is not true. People in the United States from Puerto Rico and the Dominican Republic prefer to be known as Latinos, whereas citizens from Central and South American countries prefer to be called Hispanics.

When I was a boy, "Negro" was an acceptable term, but referring to someone as "black" was unacceptable. It is the reverse today—and blacks have generated the change as well as the present preference for "African American." Similarly a person from China was once known as an "Oriental." Now the proper term is "Asian." I asked a friend, Mark Hsiao, why it is all right to refer to "Chinatown" but "Chinaman," as opposed to "Chinese man," is inappropriate. He explained that it would be the same as calling someone a "Jewman" instead of referring to him as a "Jewish man." The politically correct phrase has given us "Native American," a considerable improvement over "Indian," which geographically was inaccurate from the start.

I cite these examples because an imprecise term can negatively affect negotiations even when there is no intent at sarcasm or malice. Hot-button issues like race, religion, and political association can be off-putting to the other party if introduced in a colloquial or idiomatic manner. Today, one cannot make assumptions about the personal life of the individual in the negotiation. A lawyer who some believe is a ladies' man may be gay, or an African American lawyer may be married to a Chinese woman. My advice is to stay focused and avoid creating unnecessary detours with a nomenclature faux pas. Never criticize people's race or religion, their spouse, current significant others of either sex—or their car.

On one occasion, I was asked to sit as a kind of chairperson at a settlement conference that exemplified a poor choice of vocabulary. The husband had hired an elderly man, who was a distinguished lawyer, and the wife was using a woman in her late twenties. The older lawyer called the young woman "dear." From that moment, the discussion slid downhill. The younger lawyer chastised her adversary as being sexist and demeaning when he called her "dear." She shouted that the husband was a "two-timing adulterer," and she did not care who knew it.

I have heard male lawyers—when future calendar dates have to be arranged—say to a female judge, "I need a few minutes to call my office and ask my *girl* if I am available on that date." Judges take umbrage to this kind of sexist and demeaning language.

Jackie Mason is a larger hit in England than he is in the United States and has established a record of seven command performances for Queen Elizabeth. He also had several long-running shows (always sellouts) when he worked in London. One can imagine the difficulty the British must have experienced, trying to understand the cadence of Jackie's New Yorkese. To be truthful, even I sometimes have difficulty.

People who cannot understand what someone is saying may be too ashamed or polite to admit it. I was with Mason during a long cab ride in London when he had a conversation in incoherent double-talk with the driver. In response to the language babble, the cabdriver would respectfully interject, "Good point, sir. You're right, sir, that's exactly my opinion."

Mason also believes that people often do not listen to what he says. One time, he and I were walking in Manhattan when somebody asked for and received his autograph. Then the person kept on talking and asking questions as we continued strolling down the street. Mason interrupted the autograph seeker as we sped up our walk. He said, "I'm sorry, but I am in a hurry. My sister-in-law just jumped out of the window, and I have to get there before she lands." This autograph hound replied, "Oh, sure. Sorry to keep you."

Some name-calling is not intentionally offensive, but merely reflects historical and cultural usage. While passing through Heathrow Airport, London, a customs officer recognized Mason and said to an associate, "That's Jackie Mason, the Jewish comedian." I commented that it was objectionable to hear my close friend's profession modified with the "Jewish" adjective. Mason replied that the man's remark did not disparage the religion, stating, "That's just the way they describe people here."

To be called "Jewish" is a legitimate descriptive word in Britain. Anthony Julius, who is a distinguished English lawyer and a Jew, reinforced Mason's statements. He said to me that the British press described him as "Princess Diana's Jewish lawyer" in the same way it would have referred to him as being Scottish, Welsh, or Canadian. It seemed to have no negative connotation in the United Kingdom and he never experienced any anti-Semitic prejudice in his long and distinguished career.

If you make a purposeful pejorative comment, your adversary will take it as a direct challenge. But you do not need to ratchet up the language if a simple word or phrase will do. In referring to the husband's girlfriend, I do not have to use the words *paramour, strumpet,* or even *home wrecker* to introduce the other woman into the conversation. Notice how much more effective and less adversarial I am when I ask the husband, "And, sir, what is the name of the *person* for whose benefit you paid the bill on Room 118 at the Kit-Kat Motel?"

SLIPS OF THE TONGUE

Calculated slips of the tongue can convey information without compromising the negotiation. I can float a trial balloon and not be bound by an offhand, innocent remark. By verbalizing my comments, I avoid putting anything down in writing that could come back to haunt me.

I have used surreptitious remarks as both vinegar and honey in my legal cases. When I uncover a tax-cheating spouse who may have problems with the Internal Revenue Service (if it knew), I make it a point to caution the opposing lawyer with a furtive aside. This is unlike the disgusting practice of some lawyers, who threaten to go to the IRS if the other lawyer's client does not settle. Even if clients want their own lawyer to rat out a spouse, the lawyer should tell them, "If that's what you want, you should hire another lawyer." Or better yet, "Find a professional extortionist and then you both can go to prison."

I told one client to hire a different lawyer when I discovered he was a flagrant tax cheater. Lawyer and client confidentiality prevented me from reporting his activities to the IRS. He asked me if I would join in a four-way meeting with the wife and her lawyer to effect a settlement in a divorce case, which would include the division of large sums of unreported cash. I refused to attend such a meeting and resigned as his attorney.

A man from the Middle East brought in an order of protection that his wife had obtained against him. He said he could not understand how this had happened—he had never done anything harmful nor had he said any provocative words. I looked at the petition that accompanied the order, shocked to read that the wife swore the husband had threatened to stick a knife in her belly and rip out her innards. I looked at him aghast, and I said: "If you did this, how could you say these words? Of course, the judge gave your wife an order of protection." He stood dumbfounded, not comprehending. Then he looked at the specific threat typed out in English and translated it back into Arabic. He insisted these words were harmless and were used in his country much like, "Oh, drop dead" in this country. His native language was much more graphic and the literal translation misleadingly labeled him a dangerous person.

Another example of how different languages create confusing situations occurred when I represented Claude, son of Pablo Picasso. A lawsuit arose as a result of some gifts that his wife Sarah asserted he had given her, one of which was a small, gold nugget engraved by Picasso. The background story of this nugget was that Picasso took his son to see a local French dentist. Claude, like many young children, did not enjoy going to the dentist and became upset and tearful. Picasso asked the dentist for a piece of gold, took a dental tool, and inscribed a scene on the nugget, handing it to his son to distract him.

Another gift in this divorce case was a small Picasso drawing. Once when Claude was a boy, he became ill with the flu while Picasso was elsewhere in Europe. Whereas you or I might send a get-well-soon card, Picasso used crayons and drew a bullring with a young boy in the middle. In French, he wrote underneath the drawing, "Claude in the costume of a boy from Aragon." This was a personal treasure and not an object a husband would confer on a wife in a divorce.

However, at the deposition, when asked in English, which he spoke idiomatically, whether he promised to give his wife the drawing or the nugget, he replied, "No, not that I could recollect."

Actually, what he meant to answer was "no." But somehow, in his mind, the translation from French to English came out as, "If I don't remember the incident then my answer is 'no.'" Because of this poorly worded statement, the case was up for grabs.

I had a particular worry choosing this jury because I was concerned that jurors might be influenced by the great wealth that Claude had inherited as a result of his father's death. I was also leery that the jurors would want to touch the items so they could say they had handled a work by Picasso.

When I had used up all my challenges, I was left with a doorman from Park Avenue. I asked him the usual questions, whether the wealth or fame of Picasso would influence him in any way. He answered, "No." Then I asked my usual last query, "Do you have any questions of me?" His answer was, "Yes, who's this guy Picasso?"

The jurors deliberated and returned in 15 minutes with a verdict in favor of my client. Claude Picasso was outraged that he had been put through this nonsense when the wife's claim to the two personal items obviously was without merit. I recall that the judge in the case was more pragmatic. He said in private to me, "Well, never blame a girl for trying." That comment stuck with me for the rest of my career.

An international businessman related a similar linguistic observation. The Japanese are a deferential people and dislike to say the word "no." If you present a question to them in business terms and they want to answer in the negative, they reply with a word that means, "I understand." One can imagine what kind of havoc this sort of colloquy could cause in an American court when trying to enforce an oral contract.

THE NO WORD

A "no" puts the brakes on any discussion. It is important to find other vocabulary that does not halt the process, even though you want to turn down a proposal or end a particular line of discussion.

What I try to do is say, "That's an interesting thought. Let me think about it for a while and I'll get back to you," or, "I shall take it under advisement." This serves two purposes: It indicates that I have not rejected the idea out of hand, and it also allows the parties to move on to the next piece of business. Although my initial instincts of denying an adversary's request will probably represent my final decision, I may change my mind or find some compromise if I keep the request open for a day.

GETTING TO THE BOTTOM LINE

efore beginning any negotiations, it is critical to know what constitutes the bottom line. Often, one person in the discussion may not have thought through the process carefully enough to *have* a bottom line. This makes it difficult to have any constructive give-and-take for working toward an agreement. The game becomes a little like playing football while the goalposts are constantly moving away from you.

In divorce law with free access to both parties' financial information, the bottom line is easy to state: a fair and equitable division of assets within the guidelines set by law. If both lawyers know their business and have examined the marital finances, the magic number for settlement should have a plus or minus spread of about 10 percent.

The debate then becomes why one party is entitled to more of the soon-to-be-divided assets. I try to put myself into the head of the other lawyer and figure out my adversary's bottom line. By studying the other side, I can identify reasons to establish my client (the other spouse) in the most favorable position to gain as much as possible of the 10 percent spread. Again, the strategy is like chess where, if you play white, you had better turn the board around to understand what black will do after the opening move.

Experienced lawyers know that if the parties are antagonistic, it is prudent to avoid having the angry spouses meet at the negotiation sessions. Much of the time what a spouse wants is not an equitable settlement but rather reparations, which the law cannot grant. Animus then distorts the person's perception of a fair bottom line. Even in cases that do not appear to be polarized and the bargaining is fair and rational, the sight of the other spouse sometimes arouses volatile feelings. Before long, the situation tumbles out of control and into an emotion-packed clash. Too often—and with bad consequences—lawyers are caught up in this nonsense.

INSURANCE

Some people are unaware that insurance companies are regulated to do business in a particular state. They are required by law to set aside a "reserve," a dollar amount, for the claims made on their policies. The state wants to make sure that if the insurance company runs into financial trouble, it will have sufficient monies to cover all claims. If the company does not meet these reserve requirements, the State Insurance Commission or the State Insurance Commissioner could shut it down.

Specific aspects of reserves in the insurance business have become tax gimmicks vitiating the original intent of providing consumers with fail-safe protection. A company will manipulate the reserve requirement for its own benefit. If it books a reserve on a case at $50,000, it deducts the $50,000 reserve as an expense when it files taxes the following year. A year after that, the case is settled for $30,000, and the books now reflect an "extra" $20,000. Paradoxically, although a reserve is set aside to guarantee the integrity of the company's financial operations, if the company goes bankrupt, the reserve is treated like any other asset and becomes submerged into the bankruptcy.

Thousands of claims may be submitted at one time when catastrophes like 9/11 occur, or a massive oil spill happens on the high seas. Then the insurance companies cannot post sufficient reserves, cannot meet operating expenses, cannot pay claims, and must file for bankruptcy protection.

The key point is to know the amount in the fund and also the company's payout history, which will indicate the speed and nature of a settlement in an automobile or negligence case. This knowledge can help you assume a stronger negotiation posture. But even if you cannot learn the history of the insurance company's fund, a smart way to begin negotiation with the adjuster or appraiser is to ask knowingly, "What is the reserve on the case?" The company's representatives do not have to reveal the amount, but they often do, particularly to the lawyer who represents the claimant's interests. The amount of the reserve will suggest what the claim is worth both in terms of settlement and possibilities after litigation.

Most cities have a small group of lawyers who specialize in automobile accident claims, slip-and-fall cases, products liability, and other negligence cases. These attorneys maintain ongoing relationships with insurance companies and often have a frank and open rapport with the adjusters, which in past times—to employ a euphemism—was financial. One negligence lawyer used to list payoffs to the insurance company's adjuster as "confidential disbursements" when he sent clients a final invoice. Because of prior dealings, the lawyers can often find out the necessary information even though the reserve amounts are part of the internal working of the insurance company. By the time a case is to be tried, both lawyers know the amount of reserve on a claim, as a practical proposition after various pretrial conferences.

You can obtain the financial condition of an insurance company from the State Insurance Commission. Also, if it is a public corporation, a full report is available from the Securities and Exchange Commission (SEC). By studying these financials, you can discover whether a company is mediocre, successful, or in serious trouble. The overall financial picture affects how a particular company approaches settlements since they are interrelated with its cash flow. By studying a company's ledgers, you can sometimes estimate the size of the expected settlement.

In a negligence claim, as a threshold proposition, nothing prevents a person from suing the liable individual. The problem is that the party being sued usually does not have substantial money. It is always the insurance company that owns the deep pockets.

REAL ESTATE AND INSURANCE

I once represented a large real estate owner. To protect his interests, he bought a cheap, cut-rate policy from a little-known insurance company with a modest financial picture. That was mistake number one. Mistake number two was owning buildings in his own name instead of in the name of a corporation, which would have limited most of the exposure to the value of the buildings.

One building was a walk-up tenement. A man lived in a one-room apartment on the fourth floor and had his friend lug up an air conditioner. As they were attempting to put the air conditioner in the window, it fell out and landed on a woman who was passing underneath. The victim, a mother of three, became a paraplegic as a result of the accident. The insurance company filed for bankruptcy, knowing it did not have the reserves to pay the enormous claim.

The woman then sued my client, who had tried to save a few dollars with the low-cost insurance. He was liable for the massive verdict and was forced to negotiate. In the end, he settled the case, but because of the huge amount of money involved, he made what is called a "structured settlement," which allowed him to spread out payment of the judgment over a number of years. Not learning the bottom line of his own obligation if the insurance company should default on a claim (as it did) proved to be a costly mistake for the owner.

Building owners who never sell to developers, even at a reasonable price, are examples of people who overestimate their negotiating position. P.J. Clarke's, a New York institution, is a bar located in a rickety, one-story building on Third Avenue. Real estate operators wanted to buy P.J. Clarke's—the only building it did not own on the block—and offered the owners substantial money for the corner property. The restaurant owners refused, and today a quaint little building still houses the bar, surrounded on two sides by a towering office building.

A building in Queens, New York, is another holdout that the builder has built around and even *over*. Every large city in the United States has similar buildings that stand in tribute to owners who overplayed their hands in negotiations with real estate operators seeking to purchase their property, often at an inflated price. Perhaps these buildings also stand in silent testimony to defiance or stupidity.

Union Tactics

In 2003, the New York Transit Workers Union (TWU) contract was expiring. I followed the negotiations. I was positive that the Metropolitan Transportation Association (MTA), negotiating for the city, did not have a bona fide bottom line in mind as it entered the bargaining process. As the deadline date drew near, with the usual implied threat of a union strike, the MTA, at the final hour, caved in to most of the TWU's demands.

The cost of eventual settlement was not considered because negotiations continued without a fixed bottom line. In fairness to the MTA, having to come up with a single bottom line when a committee is attempting to formulate an agreement is like trying to add up five cowards to equal one brave man.

DEADLINES AND TIME

The bottom line will change over time as a deadline nears. If you are in the power position, the closer to a known time limit, the greater the possibility that adversaries will modify demands to your benefit. *Brinkmanship* is the name for this kind of time element bargaining. Aeronautical engineers speak of the "B moment of flight," when an aircraft about to take off has built up so much kinetic energy that it must either take off or crash. The experienced negotiator must sense, not the B moment of flight, but instead the moment before the B moment.

I use the time deadline to my advantage. If the adversarial husband in a divorce case is suspected of seeing a new woman and a holiday weekend nears, often he will be anxious to travel to some romantic retreat. I will do my best to reschedule conferences and use other delaying tactics until it is necessary to schedule the settlement meeting for a Friday. I know that on Friday afternoon the husband is likely to eschew protracted discussions, and I may be able to maneuver him into a position where he must either accede to our demands or cancel a planned weekend amatory dalliance.

Some lawyers use deadlines to make problems in the lives of adversaries. For example, some observant Jews have to be home by sundown on Friday. The lawyer then sets the meeting at noon on Friday afternoon. Another scenario is a father with a visitation schedule. Lawyers know the visitation time because they drew it up at an earlier phase of the litigation. The attorneys will schedule a meeting two or three hours before the father's visit with his children begins, placing the man in a bind. He can choose to see the children or can continue to sit in an office negotiating. As despicable as some of these ploys are, they work.

The MIRANDA Ruling

The Supreme Court's 1996 historic ruling in *Miranda v. Arizona* altered the bottom line of negotiations in criminal cases. It affirmed that law enforcement had to inform arrested suspects of their rights to an attorney, a right to remain silent, and that statements voluntarily given might be used against them. Suspects were also informed that a lawyer would be appointed, if they could not afford one.

In the days before the Miranda warning, no practical deadline of time existed to question a suspect without a lawyer present. A person then held in custody had the right to one telephone call to an attorney. But the telephone was often conveniently busy or out of order. When the person was able to contact a lawyer, law enforcement's interrogation continued while the attorney was en route to the jail to consult with the client. In addition, the suspect was sometimes shifted from jail to jail to thwart or delay the lawyer-client conference. With these devious actions, the police sometimes were able to secure confessions.

When I was a prosecutor and the *Miranda* decision first became law, the police and prosecutors were convinced that the ruling would end their ability to obtain voluntary confessions from suspects. Future cases would be made with greater difficulty without admissions from the arrested person. The supposition turned out to be false as suspects in custody proved easy to manipulate, often confessing or forgoing their rights to a lawyer. Police departments altered interrogating techniques to contend with the Miranda warning. These ploys included threats that if a suspect "lawyered up," the deal was off the table. In effect, the police said:

Confess and we can make a deal, or speak to an attorney, go to trial, and suffer the consequences of an unsympathetic jury.

When the suspect insists on seeing a lawyer, it curtails the power of the state to land a confession. In terms of negotiation, the physical presence of an attorney reduces the state's leverage and changes the bottom line in obtaining a confession. An attorney in the room advising the client will eliminate the state's potential to manipulate, coerce, or cajole a confession. The *Miranda* ruling shifted the bottom line.

THE MAGIC NUMBER

Every negotiation has a magic number. This sum represents either the maximum a person can obtain, or the most a person will have to pay in a monetary settlement.

I always create a new magic number for each process. It never hurts to start high because I can always come down to a lower amount. If I am on the receiving side, I always try to find a small opening to raise the dollar total for my client, even though both parties have access to the same financial data. Although no harm can ensue from making a high monetary request, a dollar number too high will hinder meaningful negotiation. The trick is to tempt the donkey by dangling the carrot close enough to make it want to take a bite, but not so far in front that the animal will think, "Not worth the effort."

In a recent case, where the facts supported my position, I called the other lawyer and said, "I know you and I do not agree on many points, but we are practical." This conversation was in response to a damaging deposition by his client that filled the lawyer with anger. I continued, "Don't you think we should attempt to settle the case?" His answer was, "If you do not have $10 million on the table, we have nothing to discuss." And that ended the conversation. The $10 million represented his unrealistic magic number, and the beginning of further devastating litigation against his client. The tale ends with my victory in court and his client receiving nothing.

When I am ahead of the game, I try to reach out to resolve matters. Frequently, the person in the weakened position initiates a discussion toward a settlement. But it is much better if the parties winning the argument make the first move to settle, because they are in the driver's seat. When I heard the $10 million offer, I recognized that my adversary did not want to settle; he had another agenda. He was off in left field, motivated by personal objectives that would not further his client's best interests.

In another case, my associates and I examined the specifics and decided that $4 million would represent the lowest number we would accept for our client. If we stated this sum to the other attorneys, they would assume that this represented the first demand (and not the magic number), and we would be willing to negotiate, settling for $3.5 million.

The consensus of my associates was that if we went in with a $4.5 million demand, the other side would settle for the $4 million (a fair and equitable division of assets). In the initial discussions, before settlement numbers were tossed around, I sensed that our opponents had not done their homework and had not assigned a magic number to the case. Based on my gut feelings at the meeting, I decided to be more aggressive and ask for $5.5 million. Our opponents negotiated us down to $5 million, resulting in a million more than our first reckoning.

Jeffery Shapiro, a top New York negligence lawyer, has some helpful hints on dollar negotiations:

> The style that works for me is to put everything on the table. I want the facts to determine the outcome and not my personality. Since I represent the plaintiff, I always come up with a monetary demand first. I have to state a number that is big enough that it

won't be less than the other side is willing to pay. But it can't be so high that it will stop the negotiations.

Experienced persons do not want to bargain against themselves. When shopping at the produce market, you do not say, "I will pay 75 cents for the apple." Instead, you ask, "How much is the apple?" But sometimes, even the shrewdest negotiators will let something slip in a discussion, and this should be a tip-off to their true plan.

There is a famous story about George Bernard Shaw. He was sitting next to an actress at a London dinner party and he asked her, "Would you go to bed with me if I did not have a shilling?" Her honor insulted, she replied, "Absolutely not. What do you think I am?" Then he said, "Well, I want you to think it over and tell me honestly, if I were to give you 100,000 pounds sterling to go to bed with me, would you do it?" The actress paused to consider the offer and replied, "For 100,000 pounds? Yes, I would go to bed with you." Shaw retorted, "Now that we've established *what* you are, we're just quibbling about the price."

Reasoning along these lines sometimes occurs during a meeting for a prenuptial agreement when I want to insert a "self-destruct clause" in the agreement. That unusual clause states that after a certain number of years, the agreement will be null and void and the parties will be relegated to whatever rights they would otherwise have had. Often, the husband-to-be says, "No, that's why I wanted a prenuptial agreement in the first place. I want no part of a self-destruct clause." Then I ask, "If you were married to her for 40 years, would she then have proved her worth as a wife and should obtain whatever the law would allow?" The husband replies, "Yes, after 40 years, there would be no question." I follow with, "What about a self-destruct clause after one year?" The man replies, "One year! Absolutely not." At that point, I say, "Okay, now we are just negotiating between one year and forty years."

This story is valuable for those times when you enter a negotiation without a concrete position. For example, you ask for a
raise at work, and your boss indicates that a modest raise is in the
offing. You are in the position of George Bernard Shaw: Any discussion afterward is just quibbling about price.

Hard Bargaining

I have good friends, experienced world travelers, who employ
the bottom-line approach when shopping in foreign markets
where bargaining is the cultural norm. They flew to the Middle
East to shop in Turkey and Iran. In both countries, they headed
for the most prestigious rug emporiums, where they identified
the merchandise they wanted by using an old trick of the
trade—coded negative phrases such as "this color would clash
with the couch" or "I think this size would cover too much
floor." Later, they would return to the store and begin hassling
over a midprice rug, making clear to the shop owner this was
their last day in the country. The give-and-take was always spirited because the rug merchants had had a thousand years of
negotiating practice. Once my friends struck a deal, they would
start to walk out and suddenly "notice" one of those other "less
desirable" rugs. The pretense worked like a magician's well-
rehearsed sleight of hand. By using misdirection to fool the sellers, the shoppers always walked out with the rug they wanted at
a price they were willing to pay.

On a buying trip deep into the New Guinea bush to buy
primitive masks, the husband informed his wife that the toothless,
80-year-old headhunter would trade a beautiful mask they wanted
for six goats and her hand in marriage. It was one of the few occasions where the couple did not know beforehand the seller's
bottom line.

Buyers and Sellers

I treat all sellers of merchandise as predators. Their goal is to squeeze the most profit out of the customer, and some cheaters do not care what lie or scheme they use.

I purchased at auction an Alexander Calder drawing—a charming line rendition of a nude dancer on a bridge—for a work entitled *The Book of Rats*. A client who worked as an art historian pointed out that the drawing had been mounted with Scotch tape and the adhesive had bleached through to the paper, leaving a faint but ugly stain. He offered to send it to a special art restoration laboratory for repair. About eight months later, the drawing came back with the stain miraculously gone. I kept it rolled in the cardboard cylinder in which I had received it from the laboratory.

A year later, I wanted to have the drawing appraised and decided to take it to a dealer whom I had seen on television touting the advantage of having works of art appraised by members of the prestigious National Antique and Art Dealers Association. He had a store on East Fifty-Seventh Street in New York, home to a row of famous art galleries.

Since I was moving apartments that day, I looked unkempt in old jeans and a faded sweatshirt. Under the rubric, "Clothes make the man," I did not seem like the kind of man who would know a Calder from a calzone. The staff at the gallery scrutinized me up and down and concluded that I was not an art patron. I sought out the dealer and said, "I found this drawing in my aunt's attic. I was going to throw it out but decided I should first learn if it has any value. What it is worth?" He glanced at the drawing and said with a memorable sneer, "$150 tops." I thanked him and headed for the door, concealing a wan smile.

The shop was long and rectangular and the dealer stopped me at the sales counter in the middle of the store. He had made a mistake in the appraisal. Maybe the light was bad in the rear of his gallery? He would increase the price to $500. I continued walking toward the door with him in tow beside me. More of his narrative followed; the store's cellar was full of similar looking, unsold drawings. Perhaps, if he added one more in this style, he could bundle them up and sell the lot as a package. The price vaulted to $1,000. By the time I had my hand on the door, which could end his inventive fiction, he offered $1,500. I exited the store and did not hear the next offer.

The moral of this story? First, never try to sell anything unless you first ascertain its value. Second, no matter how reputable sellers appear, it does not mean that they will pay a fair price for an item. Stores, agents, and buyers will try to make the best deal for themselves.

THE ART OF SAYING NO

Churchill observed that according to Alexander the Great the peoples of Asia were enslaved because they had never learned to pronounce the word "no."

In negotiation, there are different ways to express the "no" word. One is the disparaging method: "No, it is not worth the money," or "No, I will not give you the money." Then, there is the reverse, which says, "Yes, it is a beautiful piece. But I cannot afford it." The seller is in a bind. He cannot argue when you say the piece is wonderful. He recognizes that the person truly wants the item. Bargaining by the dealer against "I cannot afford it" is very difficult because if a buyer cannot afford $50, then to offer a terrific bargain at $49 still will not generate a sale.

If you want an item, you have to massage a "no" and cover it with layers of complimentary dialogue. In this tactic, the seller understands that the refusal is not caused by a lack of interest but by a lack of funds. At this juncture, the dynamic shifts back to the dealer who must decide how badly he wants to make a sale. The dealer will have to argue against himself.

TRADESPEOPLE

I have learned, when dealing with merchants and service workers, to say, "I would love to pay for the oak paneling, but our budget does not have room for it." How much less offensive this statement is than, "Do you think I am made of money? I wouldn't pay that much for oak paneling unless Michelangelo did the workmanship." As soon as you utter the phrase, "I won't pay that much," the merchant categorizes it as a negative remark.

Employee raises are a similar but different matter. Employees who request salary increases have a dollar number in mind and reveal it on entering the room. I do not predicate my granting of a raise on a dollar number but on how well the employee has helped Team Felder. If I feel the individual is a team player, my first reaction is to say, "The firm's budget does not allow for the size of raise you're seeking." Then I choose an amount that is lower than requested.

Lawyers in my firm sometimes have requested more money based on the number of cases they handled and how much revenue these generated for the firm. This reasoning is a turnoff for me. I have employed them to handle the workload. That is their task. If the workload were to become more than they could handle, would they expect me to reduce their salary and pay less? Or ask them to return the money I paid them under false expectations?

As an employee soliciting a raise from the boss, it helps to ask, "What was I hired to do?" and "Did I surpass what I was hired to do?" If you can answer yes to both questions, then this represents the added value of work expectations, and it should be worth more to the employer to keep a dedicated worker.

When people proffer a price for goods or services, or when employees come to ask for a raise, you have to take care in how you say "no." If you respond with disparaging comments, you will hurt the person's feelings and, perhaps, even create an enemy. If you flatly reject an employee's request for a raise, you will end up with a person taking up a workspace while searching for another job on your time.

FRANKNESS AND CREDIBILITY

It is essential to establish credibility by living up to your end of the deal when negotiating with the same people time and again. By moving off the stated bottom line, you create mistrust and condemn any further dealings with that person. The other party will be wary that, historically, your bottom line has been a sham. In the future they will believe you can be moved from the first number you quote.

An old saw reminds us that the "devil is in the details." Major and minor issues always prevail but unless *all* issues are settled, I know I will be left with a dangling problem that will plague the negotiations until we reach agreement. Imagine a company is going to deliver a load of lumber to your home. Thus, begins the list of open questions: When will it be delivered? Who is going to do the delivering? Who is going to pay the freight to have it delivered? Who is going to insure it during delivery? Details.

Inexperienced negotiators will often agree to the major points and say, "We'll work out the minor points later." What happens next is that the situation becomes unraveled because of this lack of agreement and the deal falls apart. Once I settle the major points, I make sure that no one leaves the bargaining meeting until we also agree on the minor points.

If we can accomplish the settlement in one session, it is much easier to reach agreement on the minor points since both parties are in a spirit of cooperation. But if I end the settlement with minor points not decided, I risk a different, possibly uncooperative, attitude at the next meeting. At a second session, opponents may become more confrontational on the minor points if they perceive they made a bad settlement the first time.

Experienced negotiators are familiar with the possibility of off-putting behavior at a second session. As both parties reconsider the deal, they may become unhappy with the settlement. That postsettlement dissatisfaction often undermines the resolution of minor points, and then the whole deal collapses.

An ancillary problem to an agreed-on settlement is the final step that seals the issue. A check has to be written, papers have to be drawn, somebody may need to be contacted, or something has to be delivered, adjusted, or fixed. The settlement cannot conclude without these actions. I call such items the *I do's*, signifying the vows at a wedding. If one party leaves the words unspoken, there is no official marriage.

But sometimes we never hear the *I do*; someone refuses to take the last step. This negative and destructive action makes two statements. The first communiqué is to the adversary in the negotiation, and the message is, "Fool, you cannot believe anything I say. Even if I have agreed to a settlement, you will never realize it." The second declaration is directed to the lawyer who has done the person's negotiation. It says, "I lied. I was never willing to settle."

When I find myself in this position, I prefer to resign from the case and suggest that the client hire another lawyer. If I do not step away, other lawyers will no longer trust me to negotiate a firm deal. They will think: "He will start to negotiate but then will change his mind or at least ensure the deal is never completed."

In some industries, giving one's word is bond. It is a well-known custom in the world's diamond trade that when two parties make a deal, they shake hands and say *mazel,* the Yiddish word for luck. This means the agreement is as good as if it had been written and signed. The few times diamond dealers disagree, they go to an arbitration presided over by other diamond dealers. But people in that industry trust each other's word. The custom is effective because it works, and it works because the participants stick to the deals they make—good or bad.

Some negotiators say they know a settlement was fair if both parties wake up the next day unhappy. The trouble with this philosophy is that unhappiness may translate from thought to action. Then the entire deal may fall apart.

Dealing with Indecision

Some people suffer termination anxiety and can never face conclusion. They remain always indecisive and cannot come to a final decision such as the demise of marriage or the buying or selling of a business. They are frozen—unable to end one situation and move on to another. Sensible individuals understand that life is an ongoing negotiation and renegotiated enterprise.

To avoid this indecision, when a case is settled and before pen is put to paper, I tell the client, "Go home and think about it." I emphasize that the signing is the final curtain coming down on the drama. Henceforth, they will have to live with whatever they agreed to. I have also observed that when a lawsuit is settled, a good judge questions both parties as to whether they intend to abide by the agreement.

I encounter a few people who change their minds and a settlement becomes a dance of temptation. They move toward the agreement, tantalize themselves with the prospects, and then withhold or withdraw. The best way to deal with people like this is to state: "This negotiation is not a game. Do not keep changing your mind. If you have a problem with deciding, then I cannot help you. I believe you ought to hire another lawyer—or better yet, go see a therapist."

EXAGGERATED EXPECTATIONS

Too frequently, clients in divorce cases have unrealistic expectations about the size of the settlement. This occurs even after financial data have been disclosed, and the lawyers have calculated the couple's total assets and determined reasonable expectations in the case. From the moment both attorneys know the final sum, the ultimate settlement is in plain sight with some slight variations. Some clients have more unrealistic perceptions.

I recall a divorce case in California where, as a term of the divorce, the couple agreed to trade a Los Angeles apartment and a Malibu beach house. We were prepared to go to contract to memorialize the swap, when the wife argued that the husband (my client) had installed an antique, nonworking merry-go-round behind the beach house. In addition, she claimed that he had acquired a 12-foot section of the Berlin Wall and sunk it into the ground. The total cost of the two additions was $150,000. She insisted that these items be added into the total settlement pie, imagining that she should be compensated for the additional housing improvements.

I pointed out that if the husband sold the house, he could not add onto the sales price more than $25,000 for the two additions. In fact, prospective buyers might not covet a piece of the Berlin Wall or want a merry-go-round taking up valuable space on the property.

In the library of my current apartment, the prior owner had a built-in pool table with a wooden cover that transformed it into an ordinary table. I paid nothing for this table, and since I never play pool or billiards, I sought advice on how to remove it. I have seen suburban homes for sale featuring a built-in 100-gallon aquarium, an outdoor paddle ball/tennis court, or an in-house movie projection system that did not raise the sales price one penny. No matter what homeowners believe exotic installations should add to the price of the property, the bottom line is that professional appraisers do not compute these improvements as adding substantial value to a home.

Women married to successful businessmen often overrate what they should be entitled to in a divorce. This happens when the husband's business occupation is personal service, a business that depends on the man's reputation, or one that requires his personal attendance. Lawyers place low monetary assessments on these kinds of individual enterprises.

In Los Angeles, a well-known plastic surgeon died, who was so famous in his field that heads of state and royalty traveled to see him for treatment. This surgeon did not accept monetary payments; instead he instructed patients to make a substantial contribution to his charitable foundation. For estate tax purposes, California assessed the practice at a low $50,000 since the practice did not show years of high revenues.

Yet the wife of this surgeon and the wives of other successful doctors or dentists believe that high figures should set the value of the husbands' professional practice. These women view the practice as an oil well that will continue to pump barrels for years to come, not considering that variables may cause the well to go dry.

An additional questionable area arises when a husband supports a family's high-living lifestyle by invading business capital and borrowing large sums of money from the business. When the divorce occurs, the financial reckoning by both attorneys shows that borrowing had inflated the lifestyle. The result is that the marital pie is less than anticipated, which always comes as a sad and shocking surprise to the wife.

Clients often have misconceptions about home values. It has become almost a rule of thumb that when I ask the value of an apartment or home, my client will state the price as being higher than the true market value. It is a game they play in their minds. They paid a certain price years ago and believe the value of the property has doubled, tripled, or quadrupled. Investigation will reveal that these Pollyannaish assessments are untrue.

Asset overvaluation also affects art and antiques. People have the naive impression that most works of art will increase in value over the years. Instead, most of them just get older, and their value does not appreciate exponentially with time. Some treasured antiques turn out to be nothing but old furniture with little worth.

I had a female associate whose family owned a heavy and large recast of a Frederic Remington bronze statue of an Indian on horseback. The paterfamilias, who had worked at the metal company where Remington cast his bronze works, assumed that the piece (one of three cast before the final statue was given to the sculptor) was worth $50,000. When my associate lugged this weighty piece to Sotheby's, she was informed that the rough and unsigned Remington recast had a value of $1,500, mostly for the metal.

But the winners of the overvaluation sweepstakes are the false assessments placed on the value of professional degrees or professional activities. The genesis of these overestimations began in a New York case, identified notoriously by American lawyers as the *O'Brien* ruling. The husband studied to be a doctor in Guadalajara, and the wife moved to Mexico and worked to allow him to complete medical school. Doctor O'Brien divorced his wife soon after he earned the degree.

The court put a future value on his license and practice even though he had not yet hung out his shingle. The value was computed by estimating the number of years he could practice medicine and the projected income generated to some future date. The inherent problem with the ruling was that the courts failed to consider what would happen if Dr. O'Brien should become physically unable to practice medicine or wanted to emulate Dr. Schweitzer and work altruistically in Africa. These kinds of questions, which the court did not consider, chained this doctor to chattel servitude for life.

I first became aware of the complex issue of future earnings when acting as the executor of my late brother's estate. The value put on the estate for tax purposes included unknown music royalties from future performances, broadcast plays, and record sales. Much to my surprise, no empirical data could be found to gauge the future earnings stream. What ensued became a theater of the absurd with the IRS estimating a high value and my experts predicting a lower amount. It was guesswork by both parties. The conclusion: No accurate way exists to predict what music royalties would be in the future.

But there is one appraiser whose services divorce attorneys use to calculate value. His name is Jay Fishman of Kroll Inc., and he has the talent as well as the patience to spend long and tedious hours assessing financial documents before coming up with a value for items that do not have evident value. In the Giuliani divorce, he calculated the cost of the former mayor's celebrity. He was quoted in the *Philadelphia Inquirer,* saying, "It's an intellectual challenge of putting a value on something amorphous. And what could be more amorphous than fame."

The estate of the gifted and prolific American songwriter Irving Berlin was valued in the high millions after he died. But could the courts have predicted that United Airlines would pay a fortune to use "Blue Skies" as the musical theme of its television commercials 60 years after the song was written?

Disguised Dishonesty

In some negotiations, words mean the opposite of what they are designed to convey. If you listen, you will hear adversaries sometimes giving false or conflicting signals. Once you are attuned to these words and phrases, they will alert you to a rolling bottom line that will become elusive as you try to stay on track to negotiate a settlement.

Phrases that should set off alarm signals and red flags include, "Let me be perfectly frank with you." Or, "I want to be completely honest about this." Dutch mystery novelist A. C. Baantjer wrote about his gumshoe DeKok, in *DeKok and the Naked Lady*:

> He never trusted a person who started a sentence with "to be honest." It always made him feel that honesty was such a rare quality . . . that they had to emphasize it when they were supposedly "honest." Even then, experience had taught him, they usually lied.

I have also learned never to listen to what opponents say, but instead take stock of what they do. What people do often comports with their personal history. If you have had a negative result from people you trusted, chances are that they will try to con you in the future. When they say, "We've had our differences in the past, but let's deal with this in a straightforward manner," recognize these are hollow words. These individuals are caught in the repetition of deceit and nothing will change their lies. Treat whatever follows in the negotiation with a caveat that history will repeat itself.

Once you identify a particular character trait in a person, you will witness that trait the rest of their lives. An adulterer will commit adultery and then again commit adultery. It is his nature. Wives have to accept that if they catch their husband in bed with another woman once, he will do it again, except that next time, he will be more careful. If you hire people who are sneaky or calculating with clients, they will repeat this behavior while in your employ. It says in the *Talmud*, "Not everybody who steals is a thief." But, the *Talmud* continues, "A thief steals."

DISREPUTABLE OPPONENTS

I had dealings with a person I knew to be disreputable. One element of the negotiations was that the result would be dependent on past tax returns. The tax return is a standard element in business deals where leases are keyed into profits or payments are based on income. I might request a tax return from the reputable accounting firm of Honest and Forthright, Inc. The problem is that although the firm is aboveboard and will send me a tax return prepared for the taxpayer, there is no guarantee that the taxpayer actually *filed* this particular return. The taxpayer could have given Honest and Forthright phony numbers, which the firm then included in a prepared but never sent return.

As a rule, I ask the person to sign a release for me to obtain copies of the original filed returns from the Internal Revenue Service. In the past, it took weeks or months to obtain copies of returns from the IRS. Now, however, regional offices can provide photocopies of the first pages of the return on demand. Shockingly, what you receive back as the filed tax return sometimes varies from the return first offered by the litigant or the client.

It pays to be vigilant about documentary evidence. Do not be spellbound by an official tax return, a letter from a lawyer, or certification by a well-known organization. You must go beyond these "authentic" papers.

We dealt with a lawyer whose actions and words were questionable. It was a trial in a case of a dispute over whether a prenuptial agreement would be set aside. My client, the wife, claimed she had had no counsel and was never advised of her rights. This was a key element in the case. Indeed, the lawyer she relied on was the lawyer for her ex-husband. She was unaware that she had a right to her own counsel.

The other side produced a letter from the original lawyer dated years earlier advising my client to hire her own lawyer. The letter stated that he was not her lawyer and therefore she could not rely on any advice he gave. At first glance, this letter was devastating evidence that my client had been advised of her rights and we would have to make an unfavorable settlement.

However, something bothered me about the telephone number listed on the letter that the lawyer produced. The number on the letterhead had a three-digit prefix that, to my recollection, was adopted after the date of the agreement. We contacted the telephone company. It searched records and reported that this particular prefix was not adopted until eight months after the date appearing on the letter. The lawyers had cooked up a scheme of typing a letter, back dating it, and then introducing it in evidence. However, they stupidly forgot to verify the old telephone prefix, which differed from the firm's current letterhead.

ACTOR'S STORY

Early in my career, a famous actress related an interesting story about the celebrated stage and screen actor, Paul Muni. Indirectly, it also demonstrates getting to the bottom line. In 1955, he ended a six-year retirement to assume the lead as Clarence Darrow in the play *Inherit the Wind*, which was based on the Scopes Monkey Trial.

The actress mentioned that the cast was looking forward to working with this famous actor. During rehearsals, however, Muni performed poorly, forgetting dialogue, missing his blocking, mumbling his lines, and shuffling around the stage. The cast and producers panicked that the aging actor was past his prime. The producers, already apprehensive about its theme of intolerance in American society, were now burdened with an additional concern: Could Muni deliver a forceful performance? The final dress rehearsal was a disaster. The producer and director decided to say nothing to Muni, fearing it would upset him and make matters worse.

Opening night arrived, and Muni was brilliant. The other actors and directors were astonished, and the audience was ecstatic over his performance. Muni understood his capabilities and knew that the actual performance marked the bottom line.

No Triangulation

A theme that I repeat in this book is to try to avoid third-party decision makers. This is also true for reaching the bottom line. Once you and your opponent set down the facts, the fastest route to an equitable end is to decide the matter without a third person intervening in the process.

An additional loss beyond money may be ceding power to someone who covets it. Results must be the outcome of the process. A power hungry third party may push matters to a point beyond reason.

Sometimes the third party seeks the impossible, to please everybody. There is a joke about shtetl life in the old country. Two farmers asked the town's rabbi to arbitrate a dispute about the sale of a cow. The rabbi listened to the first farmer and said, "You're right." Then the second farmer told his side and the rabbi replied, "You're right." The rabbi's student was perplexed, "Listen, Rabbi, you hear one side of the story and you say, 'You're right.' You listen to the other man's story and tell him, 'You're right.' They both cannot be right." "You're right," replied the rabbi.

My friend Howard Koeppel, who operates one of the largest Volkswagen dealerships in the United States, has established a trustworthy talented staff. Koeppel states that one reason for the contented workforce is, "I am fair and generous with them." And knowing him, I am sure he is, but his business also demonstrates the effectiveness of not using an outside instrument (the union) as a third-party arbiter. He maintains a loyal and efficient staff by negotiating one-on-one fairly with his employees. He can reach the bottom line of salary and benefits without turning the direct lines of communication into a triangle.

THE OLD COLLEGE TRY

It is more difficult to head to a bottom line in negotiations that do not require a dollar amount. An example is the discussion parents have with children about college choices. The mutual goal for child and parents is to select the best school to continue the student's education. Trying to conjure why a child has selected a college often becomes a maddening pursuit when listening to a list of institutions that may not be in the child's best interest.

The college application process is a useful example of a deadline influencing the bottom line of negotiation. The longer the parents and children delay the process, the less likely it is that they will be able to agree on where the child should apply. Delays also lessen the possibility of an admission by the college of choice.

The sensible tactic is to inquire about the reasons for your child's choice. Do this with concern, fairness, and interest. The aim for a parent in the preliminary stage is to engender a question-and-answer session that will reveal how thoroughly the child has researched the college. A student who has done detailed research should be able to give levelheaded replies. In the responses, a child may also verbalize—perhaps for the first time—interest in some future vocation.

If the student has done little or no research, then the parents have to do it, particularly, if it is a college or university that does not meet with approval. If you can cite that Lennox Valley A&M graduates a paltry 2 percent per year or forbids the use of computers and Walkmans on campus, the damaging facts start to build a negative image. It will be difficult for your child to argue for a school when confronted with such research. It is another application of the mandate that one must come to a negotiation prepared. Often a negotiation is won in the preparation, not in participation.

I have to admit that when my own two children applied to colleges, I was unable to steer either one away from schools that were not on my short list. My daughter wanted to attend a small and prestigious school in Canterbury, England, that had just started to accept women in small numbers. My son, who I had thought would attend Brown University (where he was accepted), instead opted for New York University's School of Film. My dilemma was that both children had done extensive research, and even when I presented logical counterarguments, they both held firm to the sound reasons for their selections. I had no option but to agree to my children's choices because they had the facts and answers.

Being in the Same Canoe

People often ask me: How do I know what constitutes the bottom line? And what is the best way to find it?

The answers are that in the most reasonable of worlds, you and your opponent will be in the same canoe, trying to paddle to the same place on the other side. One person is not in the canoe to go to a ball game, and the other to go to the opera. You are both trying to resolve a particular problem and then move on. The difficulty is that, because of miscalculation, the two parties may be aiming at different points on the opposite shore. The answer is to try to make sure both are heading to the same landing area. Then the argument becomes which is the best route to take.

Jackie Mason tells the story of two men who were engaged in a battle of one-upmanship. The first man shows the second man a shirt and brags he got it "at cost."

The second man replies, "I did better. I bought it at less than cost."

"How could he sell it to you at less than cost?"

"Because he sells a lot of them."

Sometimes, selling lots of shirts is the best route to take to get to the bottom line.

In legal cases, the bottom line does not result from a mysterious calculation involving complex and secretive formulas unknown to a layperson. After a financial discovery process to probe for asset and estate values, both sides should have produced an accurate and similar total. Some discussion may ensue about what each party in a divorce procedure owned before the nuptials and whether the asset became part of the marriage. However, the norm is that legal firms and their accountants are looking at the same figures.

One group of lawyers and accountants looking at a problem may reach an entirely different answer from that of another group looking at the same figures and facts. A medical practice may be valued, and one side says the practice is worth $500,000. The other side says $1 million. They both see the same set of numbers and yet come to different conclusions, looking at the same charts for what doctors should earn in certain specialties, or in specific geographic areas. In one case, a doctor did not work the full 40-hour week as anticipated in the published figures valuing medical practices. Therefore, to determine what his practice was worth, the figure had to be extrapolated upward to indicate the level that it would be if he worked 40 hours.

A case I tried involved a man whose business was the importation of steel. The forensic accountant that the wife hired produced substantial figures, culminating in his testimony that the business was worth a high number. The accountant who testified was reputable and well meaning, but he did not do his homework. Steel that is imported into the United States is subject to quotas and taxes, or duties. The price that a person pays for imported steel depends on the quotas and duties that the federal government establishes under a complicated mechanism, and these costs vary from year to year.

Although the wife's accountant did the necessary research in the case, he neglected to compute these duty and tax variables that change annually. When I discovered this inaccurate accounting, I asked that the judge strike the accountant's entire testimony. The judge had a dilemma; the case was two years old and it would mean knocking the wife right out of the box and not giving her a day in court. The judge "reserved his decision" as to my request, which means he would decide the issue of whether the testimony by the wife's expert would be admissible at the end of the case. The wife, seeing the handwriting on the wall and understanding her predicament, allowed a quick settlement to ensue.

Lawyers see differences of valuation, particularly in real estate. One party may use a qualified real estate appraiser who will write a report stating that a property is worth $500,000. Then, a second appraiser will say the property is worth $800,000. Homeowners do not know which appraiser to use.

On occasion, real estate appraisers do not use the correct number of square feet in valuing a parcel. In a recent case, the appraiser saw vacant land behind the house that he thought could be built on, which would make the property less desirable. What he did not realize was that it was a wetland protected by law.

In the midst of the Scull art case, a question arose as to the value of a house they owned in Connecticut. Since Ethel was going to be awarded the property, it was in Robert Scull's interest that it be valued high and Ethel Scull's interest that it be valued low.

Robert Scull produced an appraiser who testified to what I perceived was a large and unrealistic value for the land. He tried to make the case that since a cemetery was located behind the property, these burial grounds would always remain pristine and undeveloped. He was sure that the open space would add value to the property and also provide Ethel with an appealing view. I asked the man archly, "And who besides Dracula and other vampires would want to live next to a cemetery?"

The bottom line is to accept no expert judgment in any matter unless you examine and verify the individual facts that make it up, and study the components of that professional's judgment. A conclusion is only as good as the sum of its parts. And that's the bottom line.

PHYSICAL CONDITIONING

A t the end of the nineteenth century, a Greek politician said, "England always wins one battle—the last." The comment says less about bravery than about a commitment to continue fighting until the war is won.

All negotiation is adversarial. And some negotiations will test your physical as well as your mental capabilities. You have to be equipped to deal with the strain of a long negotiation or you will fail to achieve your goal.

How often people say, "He wore me down," or "They wore me out." Or a mother says to a father at the end of the day that she gave their children permission to play outside and not do homework because "They wore me out." It is an admission of losing for lack of physical endurance. People capitulated because they were exhausted by the long-lasting struggle and could not continue.

In my youth, I could stay up the entire night for lengthy legal negotiations because I required very little sleep. I could wear down adversaries who were yawning or even falling asleep at the table while I was making points. No one else wanted to go on butting heads into the night.

So frequent were my all-nighters that I came to know by sight and name the late-night cleaning persons for our offices. They numbered among those mysterious Eastern European women who seem to have the unwritten franchise for cleaning Manhattan's office buildings. These workers are seldom seen by anyone except people traveling the subways to work at 6 A.M. when the women are returning home after their all-night jobs.

It was common for my secretaries to come into my office in the morning and see papers everywhere, many half-empty coffee cups, and ashtrays filled with cigarette butts. The secretaries always wondered why the Albanian cleaning crew had bypassed my untidy office.

In the past few years, I have halted this stay-up practice. It is grueling on body and soul. The law has changed, with its emphasis on facts, and although I still have the capacity to stay awake and argue until the dawn, it is more difficult to find lawyers or even clients with the same desire or endurance.

In the recent MTA New York City negotiations, I am sure that the union's negotiators wore down management in the deliberation process. The union team is accustomed to gearing up for an extended process and is used to spending long hours for deliberations, catching a few hours of sleep, and wearing the same clothes until the contract is settled. But management has no such experience for the long haul. It is represented by skilled executives who are paid well, but not for their ability to sit up all night in a smoke-filled room, engaging in arguments and discussions. The union will win if staying power determines the outcome.

No Food, Please

The new wrinkle in evening discussions is ordering food. If I know ahead of time that my opponents want to call in a meal, I will excuse myself and reschedule. My close friend Jackie Mason speaks a truism; an entertainer cannot compete with food. I have often heard him tell young performers that no matter how great an act they have, it will not be able to compete with a room full of waiters serving a meal.

Food as a distraction upsets long settlement conferences. First, everyone scans the takeout menu, discussing the choices. Then, what follows are orders so detailed that only an experienced waiter could write down the permutations: "Rare but not too rare, mayo on the side, baked potato but hold the sour cream, half-and-half and not milk, no whipped cream on the pudding . . ."

Once the food order has been called in, the subconscious desire for the food supersedes concentration on the discussion process. The meals arrive, and someone will start distributing hot and saucy dishes, inquiring, "Who had the Stroganoff? Who asked for the extra order of kale?" The food sorting over, the conference table is now full of dishes, utensils, and, on average, about a thousand more napkins than necessary. And the place smells like a delicatessen. Woe to the restaurant that forgets an item. Then it is, "Call up now. They forgot my peach melba."

No business will be discussed during the eating of food. Food ordering is a distraction and should be avoided. Once everyone is bloated from eating, the pace of a long conference slows down to a crawl; and soon everyone wants to pack it in and call it a day. I often advise young lawyers, "The blood is either in your head or your stomach." In negotiations, it has to stay in the head. When you have a full meal, it goes to the stomach and the head suffers.

Jury Trials

A jury trial is a good example of negotiation for the long haul. Jurors may take hours and even days to deliberate in spirited and heated debates about guilt and innocence. But what happens at the end of a long day or a series of days is that people lose the ability to continue. Their resistance has been worn down, and they have less stamina for argument. Many verdicts arise because a jury is exhausted and cannot prolong the deliberations. The jurors are tired and want to go home.

Jury service is an example of the negative reaction to a long process. When a judge announces to prospective jurors that the case could last six months, many people on the panel will try to be excused. A gripe I hear from my staff when they are called for jury duty is, "I did not know it would last so long."

Other Lawyers

Similarly, if a Wall Street firm—or what we used to call a "white-shoe" law firm—is on the other side, these lawyers are used to working an eight-hour day and then going home, making them raw meat for the average divorce attorney. We are prepared to start our day when the Wall Street lawyers are on their way home. The divorce specialist is prepared to argue about matters small and large in areas tangible and arcane that the Wall Street lawyer would not think worthy of the time, especially if that time is after the normal work hours.

In any large law firm in a major city, lights burning until the early morning hours signify late-night workers. But if you venture into the offices, you will never see any of the people with heavy responsibilities. Inside are young lawyers with heads buried in books, or teams of secretaries doing nighttime assignments.

A spear is only as good as its point. In a Wall Street firm, at 10 o'clock at night, the corporate lawyers who should form that point are not in the office doing research or working on briefs. For a protracted negotiation, whether in the divorce area or another domain, an experienced lawyer who is the point of the spear may still be on target at 10 o'clock at night, and long after, working for resolution.

Never Tip Your Hand

At the beginning of a negotiation, it is a mistake to announce, "I think that these talks will last about three months." You have tipped your hand as to how long the process will take. The serious error is that opponents will mark 90 days down on their calendar for the real end-of-settlement deliberations. They will disregard the weeks leading up to the final week at the end of the third month. Then they will begin negotiating in earnest.

It is much better to let adversaries believe the end of the negotiation is much closer than it is. Then the other side starts making plans for vacations or other casework. When arranging their schedule, they anticipate a timed chronology with an appropriate beginning, middle, and end. But you can upset the scheduling applecart if your negotiations go beyond the time originally allotted to this process. You may be able to expedite a better settlement because adversaries will have planned for an ending according to their time frame, not yours.

To determine how long a meeting might last, I look for little clues from my opponents. If I see adversaries toting several bottles of water into the conference room, I know they are gearing up for a long struggle.

Profile of Opponents

I also like to find out where opponents live and whether they go home by taxi or train to the suburbs. I know from experience how long it will take to travel to almost any out-of-town destination. The information gives me a good idea when my adversary will want to leave the field of battle. I can find out the necessary information by asking if they will need my office to call a taxi to take them home. Even in declining my offer, they will reveal their address.

When gearing up for a negotiation, the thought is, "This work is going to take me until midnight or 1 A.M. to finish." The inference is that you will still be alert at 10, 11, or 12 o'clock at night. If you think, "I will finish this by 7 P.M.," however, your body mysteriously signals tiredness at 6:45 P.M.

STRATEGIES

In any negotiating process, develop a feel for the right time to call it a day. I try to determine the number of objectives I want to accomplish during the discussion session. If I believe that we can agree on two, then when these two are resolved, I leave the table saying, "We have settled points A and B and I think that should be sufficient for the day."

I have found that accomplishing three major objectives during one conference is pushing the envelope. To pursue more than three goals is folly. The smart play is to stop when ahead.

In a divorce case, let us assume that two of the six or seven major items may be who will have the summer home and who will pay the children's college costs. If, out of the major items, I can complete these two items without leaving any loose ends or any minor details, then I can end the conference and resume talks another day. However, if there are bells and whistles and conflict about these two points, then the process will collapse. An item must be complete in every respect before I go on to the next one; the trick is finding subjects that offer a quick resolution.

LAWYERS AND JUDGES

In days past, some judges would say (and these were perhaps the best judges), "No one leaves the courtroom until we come to an agreement." The lawyers then knew they were in for a long deliberation. Today, the law has changed, and judges are under constraints not to be arbitrary or dictatorial with attorneys and litigants. Lawyers can make complaints about judges to the authorities and judges are constantly monitored, causing the circle to come around and create a body of judges who do not take a firm hand in resolving cases. This new accommodation signifies fewer marathon sessions.

If I meet older lawyers, I know that they will have less vigor for the long fight, with shorter attention spans, and will rely on their reputation to sustain them in the discussion. When I negotiate with some older colleagues, I am reminded of the line from the A. E. Housman poem, "Runners whom renown outran, And the name died before the man."

Final Words

Know the physical condition of your adversaries. Know their strengths, weaknesses, and limitations. Remember, younger opponents will have more stamina.

However, I have never found a situation where cunning, guile, and experience were not more than a match for youthful vigor. Because in the last analysis, negotiation is not a horse race or an endurance test, it is an arena where experience and insight into human nature carry the day.

12

ACTING CRAZY

Acting crazy is both an effective strategy and a useful fallback plan when the normal path to negotiations becomes stalled or blocked. The simple truth is that no one wants to deal with a lunatic.

Reflect on those times when you were walking down a street and spotted a bag lady mouthing vulgarities. Or you encountered a down-at-the-heel man wearing a Bozo the Clown wig, dancing on the sidewalk, and singing, "I gotta be me." What did you do? Without thinking twice, you moved to the other side of the street. These weird people caused discomfort, and it seemed prudent to avoid them.

In negotiations, it is possible to gain the upper hand by resorting to odd behavior. A strange act, a bizarre response, or an out-of-the-ordinary glance can startle a lethargic or slow-moving meeting into surprised shock. You will have but one shot to employ this approach in the course of the discussions.

As a ploy, the outlandish act serves two other positive purposes; it redirects the spotlight on you, and it may cause adversaries to become uneasy about further dealings. In effect, you are trying to break up your opponents' rhythm by diverting attention away from them to you in one swift, unanticipated move.

On my office wall is a certificate of appointment to the Department of Justice signed by Robert Kennedy, along with a plaque commemorating my retirement from the Department. With that judicial backdrop, when I rant and rave about the indecency of a person not paying his taxes (and the fact that we—the honest taxpayers—all have to share the deadbeat's obligations), my opponents in a case with such tax elements may begin to think that I am a wild man who considers himself to be an avenging angel of justice.

In reality, any concerns they may have are unwarranted, since as an attorney, I am under an obligation of silence and cannot violate my oath in relation to past, tax-cheat criminal acts to which my client, as a spouse, was a party. The record will show that I have never threatened to take actions of this disreputable kind.

Fish Frenzy

I represented a wife in a divorce whose husband owned a chain of pet shops in the metropolitan area. They proceeded amicably to a settlement and I became friendly with the man, who bore no grudge against me for handling his spouse's divorce.

One day, we were discussing the pet business, and I asked if it was possible for him to find flesh-eating piranhas. I knew that selling piranhas was illegal in New York State but owning them was not. The pet shop owner located the piranhas from another state and set up a 50-gallon aquarium in my conference room. The aquarium contained plastic plants since the nibbling fish would tear up live ones. Everyone in the office was instructed to keep hands out of the tank. A maintenance man did any necessary plant and gravel restorative work by using two sticks, since if he used his hands, the fish might use his fingers for an appetizer.

I began to consider how these pet fish could help out during conference meetings.

Piranhas need live fish to eat, which are called "feeder gold-fish" in the trade. Although the piranhas do not have to be fed every day, dry flakes of fish food will not provide the same nutrition as live fish with their protein-laden body parts. When the small goldfish are dropped into the tank, the piranhas attack them, making a loud, biting *crunch*. A sort of piranha tummy burp follows the meal and makes a visible bubble as it rises to the water's surface.

In terms of predator and prey, the sight of a live goldfish being attacked is more upsetting to some people than a cat toying with a dead mouse or a fox terrier shaking the head of a rat. The goldfish is swimming one minute and is lunch the next. The attack is swift, sharp, and final. Not a sight for the queasy.

During heated conferences, I make it a point to feed the piranhas. Since in some circles I have the reputation of being a shark, the piranha attack reminds my adversary that I also could make a *crunch* sound.

Mr. Loony

Years ago I represented a woman from upstate New York in a divorce case. Her husband, a successful real estate entrepreneur, owned much of the land surrounding a large hospital complex in a New York suburb that was the satellite location of a well-known New York City hospital. He had amassed a fortune by building housing for the staff and selling off parcels of land to the hospital when it needed to build additional facilities.

He earned the dubious but deserved nom de plume of Mr. Loony. This genuine eccentric had achieved wealth and fame by a series of odd but useful behaviors. He insisted that real estate closings occur in his Manhattan office. If a disagreement arose, he rushed into an office closet. His adversaries had to consider whether he was an unbalanced dolt with a screw loose, half a crackpot, or just a tad touched in the head. In any event, they had to deal with and obtain a signature from a person who had disappeared into a closet. He would bawl that the other side must agree to his terms or he would remain in the closet. It unnerved opponents, and Mr. Loony succeeded more often than not.

These victories spurred the man to additional weird and wonderful actions. He shaved the hair off one side of his head. In fact, he had special hats made that covered only one side of his head when he went out in public. Again, it is not a rhetorical exercise to ask, "What course of action would you take if you walked into an office for a business meeting and spotted a man with the hair shaved off one half of his head?" The half-hairy head attracted unremitting stares as a bright candle attracts moths to dance around the flame.

It is disconcerting to see a businessman dressed in a conservative shirt, tie, and suit, with half of his hair shaved off. No matter how well prepared a person is to negotiate a deal, the process will take a backseat to new thoughts: "Is this guy crazy or what? What do I have to be afraid of? Can I make any sort of a deal with this nutcase?" What happens is the negotiation becomes solely his agenda. Your goal is to complete the business dealings and exit as soon as possible.

Liz Trotta

One of my own acting-crazy stories proved to be the perfect tactic to right an egregious wrong when the CBS network fired journalist-reporter Liz Trotta. She had been a pioneer in broadcast journalism, the first female television war correspondent, and the first woman to cover the Vietnam War. She also prepared excellent stories on the Kennedy assassination, the Israeli Yom Kippur War, the Iran hostage crisis, and the invasion of Grenada.

Her on-air reporting earned three Emmys and two prestigious Overseas Press Club awards.

Trotta had to battle the discrimination that hedged in woman journalists as broadcasters. She had to fight for respect, overcoming constant humiliations from the male-dominated media culture. One time in 1967, while working at WNBC in New York, she was asked to do a piece for the NBC network, an opportunity for much envied national exposure. The fluff topic was to report on Lynda Bird Johnson's wedding dress. She refused, saying indignantly, "I do not do weddings."

In 1985, CBS signed Trotta to a long-term contract to work for its News Division. Then, at the age of 41, she was canned—booted out into the street. In addition to bad economic times in the television industry, internecine battles in the CBS News Division pitted older, hard-line journalists, who were veterans of the prestigious Edward R. Murrow news years, against the new, profit-at-all-costs management. The latter began a purge of the News Division with a rash of firings.

The CBS bloodbath became a choice morsel for the media. After I read about it in the newspaper, I contacted Trotta, whom I knew. The firings may have appeared to be the long overdue sacking of senior employees with big salaries. Some Wall Street media analysts viewed the terminations as necessary cost-cutting moves—and maybe they were. But I sensed that Trotta, who was female, a political conservative, and older, may have received the axe for more discriminatory reasons. From a legal perspective, she had a few months earlier signed a long-term contract that bound her services to CBS. At first glance, it seemed like a breach-of-contract issue. However, I believed it was more sinister. From CBS's viewpoint, she was too old and too smart, and a journalist in the finest sense of that word. The cost-cutting executives also may have thought that her deal was too rich an item. Alas, the current fashion then and since in female newscasters has been to hire perky cheerleader types who read rather than write the news.

I volunteered to pursue some remedy for Liz Trotta without charge. My gut feeling was that a serious wrong had been committed and I wanted to redress it. I thought that if I could talk in private with a lawyer at CBS, I could resolve the matter in a more favorable settlement for Trotta. Maybe, at the very minimum, I could negotiate an increase in the amount of the severance, providing her with a longer income bridge into the future until she could find a new job.

After a few telephone calls, I found a CBS attorney who was willing to listen to my request to discuss Trotta's circumstances. He scheduled a meeting at the network's headquarters. On the day of the appointment, I walked over to the familiar Black Rock building on West 52nd Street. I anticipated an informal engagement, the casual kind that attorneys are good at, with give-and-take that would allow both sides to reach a fair and reasonable middle-ground agreement.

But instead of meeting a CBS lawyer in an office, I was surprised to be ushered into a large conference room. Seated around a long conference table were almost all of CBS's board of directors (a collection of distinguished *éminences grises*), other senior network executives, and a few in-house attorneys. A rough count indicated that there were about 15 men in the room, all eyes staring disapprovingly at me. It seemed as though I was appearing before one of those covert star chambers made up of prominent, judgmental, and powerful people.

At that moment, I had one of those flashes of insight that occurs when a large amount of data is processed into one raw emotion: I was being set up to be sandbagged! In effect, I was to playact the misbehaving schoolboy called to the CBS docket to suffer a lecture and censure not just by the principal but also by the entire school board.

My instincts cried out that polite or lawyerly behavior would accomplish next to nothing for Liz Trotta. The CBS network had displayed profound contempt for her reputation as an eminent journalist and for me as an attorney. It had mounted a potent show of force to intimidate her and buttress the reasons for the termination. The all-male crowd represented overkill, and it seemed unchivalrous that these men would publicly attack an award-winning woman reporter who was given one day to clean out her office.

My blood boiled, and then it boiled over. No sooner had someone in the room made an innocuous introductory statement, than I began the mother of tirades. I cursed with words that I had not used since schoolboy days. I was outraged. I ranted. I raved. I promised the board that before the day's end, every newswire service, every television station, every newspaper, would know how CBS treated loyal female employees—that a contract with the network was worthless—that the company would not honor their commitments. The world would learn of the network's hypocrisy.

Then, I continued the vehement attack along legal lines, citing the network's flagrant and callous contempt for the employment contracts it signed. Shouting at the top of my lungs, I said, "You #@%*#* want war? I'll give you war. I will litigate until this Black Rock turns pale." I threatened a class action suit against CBS and the individuals in the room on behalf of the newly terminated employees. I stormed out of the room.

Later that day, back in the office, Liz Trotta called to say she had just gotten off the telephone with a CBS lawyer. He was astounded that such a dignified woman had hired a crazy person to represent her against the network. My histrionic performance had shocked the board of directors. There was an unfortunate misunderstanding. The last thing it wanted was to seem ungenerous.

The upshot was that CBS renegotiated her puny severance. It bought out her contract for two full years, stipulating that she could not work for another network in that time. She accepted the terms and used those two years to write an engrossing, well-reviewed autobiography called *Fighting for Air*, published in 1991. Today, she writes a column for the *Washington Times* and appears on the cable Fox News channel.

PERIPHERAL CRAZINESS

Sometimes unexpected craziness during the negotiations will have a beneficial effect in resolving a dispute. An improbable event—one that you cannot plan or anticipate—will help determine the result.

In 1968, I represented a stockbroker that the Internal Revenue Service accused of tax violations. The agency knew that he was a co-owner of a hole-in-the-wall Swiss bank. He wanted to cop a plea but would not accept one unless it was preagreed that he would serve no jail time.

The IRS agreed that if he would find out details about the modus operandi of American citizens who opened secret Swiss bank accounts and funneled monies into Switzerland, it would let him off with a fine and no jail time. The agency insisted that my client had to produce documents from certain Swiss banks and also had to tape useful conversations with Swiss banking personnel.

I advised him to accept this offer. However, I knew that it was a crime in Switzerland to discover information secretly about the country's confidential banking operation. At least it was a crime if perpetuated in Switzerland, where violators could be arrested and jailed. The IRS was unmoved by our legal dilemma and insisted that the taping occur or else my client would find himself behind bars. The alternative was to arrange a meeting with a Swiss banker outside the country where that nation's laws would not apply.

The stockbroker chose Czechoslovakia with the full consent and sanction of the IRS. A Swiss banker consented to meet him in Prague after my client promised to do more substantial business with the bank in the future. Coincidentally, I was taking a deposition in Paris at the time. I requested that the stockbroker keep me informed on the preparations for the meetings. I wanted to review beforehand the steps he would take to ensure that the script met the terms dictated by the IRS.

We scheduled a mid-morning telephone call from Prague to my Paris hotel room on the day of his meeting. We were reviewing point after point for his lunch with the banker when abruptly he said that he heard loud noises outside his window and dropped the phone. I heard a series of ear-piercing booms that sounded like lightning and thunder. Was it a violent storm?

In a few seconds, he returned to the telephone. Panic-stricken, he shouted, "Tanks! You won't believe this but I see Russian tanks in the street." It was the first day of the Soviet Union's defiant response to the Czech uprisings. I told him to check out (no pun intended) of the hotel, head to the American Embassy, and exit the beleaguered country by any means possible.

"What about my banker's meeting?" he cried out. "If I do not meet this guy, I am going to jail." I said personal safety should be his first priority; the meeting could wait.

When I returned to New York, I contacted the IRS and described in detail my client's valiant efforts to acquire the information required by the bureau. I evoked the morning in Prague with its peril, imitating some of the great on-the spot, radio correspondents of World War II like Robert Trout and Edward R. Murrow. Here was my client, alone and in danger, trying to carry out a noble mission for the Stars and Stripes. Here arrived the Russian tanks, clamoring down the streets, firing into buildings. I suggested that under these horrifying circumstances the agency's actions, unknowingly, had placed an American citizen in harm's way, but we had no interest in revealing this fact to the public. Perhaps, I suggested, it would be sensible for the IRS to forgo seeking that last pound of flesh in my client's sentencing. I urged the agency to let this small potato plead guilty, pay a fine, and avoid prison. The IRS consented. My client served no jail time because of the political craziness in Czechoslovakia.

WEIRD AND OUT-OF-CONTROL JUDGES

In the 1979 film *And Justice for All*, the great actor Jack Warden played an over-the-top, oddball judge who waved a pistol around the courtroom. The film was a dark, sardonic look into the American justice system, starring Al Pacino as a principled attorney. The judge's weird behavior in the film might have seemed like ingenious cinema fiction to a layperson, but to attorneys whose lives are spent in courtrooms, the Warden character's behavior resembled the sometimes—though infrequent—awful truth.

Most judges try to be as fair as possible although they are miserably underpaid and overworked. Some, however, are legitimate crazies or have legitimate emotional problems. This fact should not surprise anyone since there are tens of thousands of judges of every stripe and every age presiding over the municipal, state, and federal judiciary systems. Statistically, very few of these judges exhibit behavior not in keeping with the decorum of normal judicial conduct.

A judicial madness occurred in Long Island. A judge became annoyed as, day after day, a licensed hot dog vendor's loud spiel for "A hot frank with everything" filtered into the courtroom through an open window. The judge finally became so irritated he ordered the vendor arrested.

In my own career, I remember two particular instances. A prospective juror wanted to sue a Bronx New York State judge for ordering him removed from the courtroom accompanied by a bailiff and held in a cell. During questioning by the judge about the man's possible recusal from the case, the pair had started a colloquy that erupted into a shouting match. The outraged judge ordered the man placed in handcuffs, removed from the court-room, and taken to a holding cell. Picture this: A citizen comes to court to do his duty and winds up in a dank jail cell.

Police officers waiting in the court to testify were so put off by the judge's action that one of them complained to Administrative Judge Burton Roberts, who had been a top-notch and well-respected prosecutor with extensive knowledge of the limits on the powers of the judiciary. Judge Roberts convinced the trial judge to undo what he did or face possible judicial censure. The irate judge called the man back into court and said if the man would apologize for his conduct, the judge would apologize for his. And that is what happened.

I had to disappoint this juror since he stood no chance of prevailing in a suit for false arrest or false imprisonment. Judges have wide-ranging immunity from prosecution for actions they take in the courtroom. Judges need great latitude in presiding over cases, because if fear of censure or of being sued intimidated them, they would pamper attorneys and witnesses to the detriment of the legal process.

At one time in New York County, as in many other counties in the United States, a judge had to listen to routine testimony before granting an uncontested divorce. The parties would have previously made financial and other agreements, and the divorce itself was conducted pursuant to a virtual script. Frequently, a clerk would hand the lawyer the 12 or 13 questions that the witness—husband or wife—had to answer and then the judge would say, "Divorce granted. Next case." But with the increase in the divorce rate, even this rapid one-stop process became time-consuming and now divorce is granted "on papers."

In New York County, there was a judge who had an excellent reputation in the intelligence department, but a less than adequate one concerning his temperament. The papers were signed, and the time arrived for the couple to answer the choreographed questions in order for the judge to grant a divorce.

In this particular case, after the questions, before the judge said his usual "Divorce granted," he called the lawyers to the bench and said to us, "The husband looks like a fag to me." He referred the matter *sua sponte* (a legal term that means "of their own accord") to the court's family counseling unit to write up a report on the custodial situation. We were shocked and outraged. After the counseling unit's report came in, the judge took it upon himself to write a decision. He disguised the names of the parties, but kept otherwise identifiable elements in the decision. When the local press ran the story, the husband's colleagues recognized his identity. Justice prevailed in the long run; I read in the media that as a result of an official complaint by the husband, an investigation ensued and this homophobic judge was kicked off the bench.

CRAZY LIKE A FOX

There are occasions when playacting the dumb bunny in a negotiation can give you the upper hand. This will hold true in contractual talks where an adversary is accustomed to repetitive and often boring bargaining patterns. When you realize that your spiel will be the same old speech, adding an unusual twist can work to an advantage.

A Los Angeles lawyer had a client who was a famous, award-winning screenwriter. The man had previously signed and completed a standard three-picture deal, and his contract was up for renewal with a major Hollywood motion picture studio. The studio had hired a tough bargaining attorney with a take-no-prisoners reputation to head its talent contract division. Talent agents feared this new attorney, who prided himself on tough, toe-to-toe bargaining and who relished saving money in brutal contract negotiations.

The lawyer was astounded to learn from his staff that the screenwriter did not use the services of an agent or a business manager. Instead the writer represented himself in contractual negotiations. The lawyer looked forward to this meeting as a wolf might relish welcoming a lamb to dinner. He decided to lowball the offer for another three-picture deal, counting on years of exacting negotiating skills to refute the writer's anticipated demands for more money.

The lawyer salivated with delight when the screenwriter walked into his office alone. After a few cordial remarks, the studio executive handed the writer a single piece of paper with the proposed fees that the studio would pay for contract renewal. The writer glanced at the offer for a moment and then said, "This is a wonderful offer. It's very generous of the studio."

The lawyer beamed with satisfaction. This would be the fastest signing he had every experienced. The studio would gain the services of a celebrated screenwriter at a substantially below-market cost. He asked, "Would you like to sign the contract now?"

The screenwriter smiled, saying, "I would. But first I have to show it to my *client*."

The lawyer was dumbfounded. "Your client?"

"Yes," said the writer, "I am here today in the capacity of his agent. And if it were up to me, I'd have my client sign this exceptional offer. But it's not up to me. It's up to him."

"Him?"

"Yes. And although I would be honored to take this magnanimous offer to my client, I know that with his oversized ego, he might reject it out of hand."

The lawyer had no other choice but to play along. "He might? Why?"

"The guy reads the trade papers. He's jotted down the large grosses generated by his scripts. He's been around this town long enough to know that money talks."

The lawyer started to enjoy the charade; it was a different gambit from the standard combative agent's spiel. He was amused by the audacity of the writer's playacting. The dialogue continued along the lines of the "agent" badmouthing his "client" until the attorney rolled with laughter.

The lawyer asked, "Okay, what would it take for your client to sign with the studio?"

The writer handed over a piece of paper with a number written on it. He said, "In my humble opinion, he doesn't deserve half of this amount. But who am *I* to say?" And the lawyer ordered his staff to draw up a contract for that amount of money.

The writer's brilliantly planned and crazy shtick had succeeded where an actual agent might have failed. For years, the studio executive enjoyed recounting the story of meeting the crazy agent and his client.

CRAZY LITIGANTS

Lawyers will assert that the worst-case scenario in their practice is to represent a litigant who acts daffy or dotty. I find that I cannot make a deal with a client for whom I cannot negotiate in good faith. Like other attorneys, I throw up my hands when confronted with an authentic eccentric or an unbalanced personality.

Look for tip-offs that reflect or at least suggest a person is living in an unreal world. Red flags go up when clients talk about strange people following them, telephones being tapped, and their mail being opened and read. Henry Kissinger said, "Sometimes, even paranoids have something to be paranoid about." But people are certifiably insane when they narrate tales about rays coming from Ming the Merciless of the planet Mongo, or Elvis Presley tunes being played through the gold fillings in their teeth.

I had a client who claimed "they" were beaming rays at her head. She refused to visit a psychiatrist and instead hired a private detective to shadow her. The detective called me from her apartment and said that everything was under control. He told the woman to wrap herself in tinfoil, which would protect her from the rays. She followed his advice and at home greeted guests clad from head to toe in Reynolds Wrap.

Sometimes there is no way to deal with a person who operates under the delusions of paranoia. I had a client who was convinced a certain person was poisoning his food and beverages, and he lost a lot of weight because of this fear. I suggested that he drink canned soda but he refused, stating, "This individual is so powerful, he entered the bottling companies and poisoned the contents of the cans." I bought him a tabletop water distillation apparatus, which he used for only a few days before insisting that the omniscient individual poisoned the water, too.

Manic-depressives with cash fly high and dive deep. I had one case where a rich man in a manic phase drew up plans to build a huge, underground mausoleum next to a major highway in Canada. Above the mausoleum, at ground level, he planned to build a gourmet restaurant whose slogan would be: "Visit your loved ones and enjoy a great meal." He hired an architect who drew plans for the burial bistro, but the Canadian officials rejected the project.

Crazy Lawyers

From time to time, lawyers on my staff will meet an attorney who manifests odd or off-putting behavior. My advice to them is twofold: Allow them to talk until they stop, or better, cut off discussions. I can handle adversaries who curse at me. And I can barely tolerate the gimmicky attorneys who use legal parlor tricks to delay or hinder the process. But I am impatient with irrational conduct.

Lawyers, like anybody else, can develop mental illnesses, and when they are in the throes of such problems, they can become abusive with adversaries. Thrust meets counterthrust, and aggression meets aggression.

We had a case in which the opposing lawyer had an obvious mental condition and was becoming antagonistic for no reason. One of my lawyers—a former social worker with years of dealing with similar situations—calmly said, "Breathe deeply and relax. We'll end this conversation. Then take a pill and we'll talk again in fifteen minutes." This advice worked to perfection; the man medicated himself, rested awhile, and the case proceeded without the craziness.

MA, MA, WHO'S THE PA?

I represented a married man who denied paternity of a child in his marriage. It is very difficult to obtain a court order for a child's blood tests while the mother is married. Indeed, it is axiomatic that "the strongest presumption in the law is that of legitimacy." My client was a strapping blond-haired, blue-eyed man in his mid-thirties. He assured me that the boy was not his own even though the child also had blond hair, blue eyes, and, exhibited similar facial features. The husband proposed that if the wife would submit the child to a blood test—and it turned out that he was the father—he would pay her double the support awarded. Or, if the blood test proved he was not the father, he would pay her nothing.

I asked my client how could he be so certain that the child was not his. He responded, "I heard it from the living God." It was clear to me that he was a nutcase. I followed his instructions, however, and the wife agreed to the double-or-nothing deal and signed papers. Unbeknownst to me, the wife tried to hedge her bets by conducting a test using her blood and the child's blood. Although any test without a sample of my client's blood would be inconclusive, she had gone to a second-rate local laboratory that provided a report she interpreted as proving my client was the child's father.

Finally, a blood test was performed at a reliable laboratory. The analysis remained sealed until both parties were in my office. I opened the report, and it stated that my client was not the father. In those days, I had one of those funny coconut heads on my desk decorated with eyes and teeth made out of embedded seashells. After we read the shocking report, the wife became so white-hot angry that she smashed the coconut shell over my client's head, rendering him unconscious.

The wife and her lawyer fled the office. Paramedics were called in, and they placed my bloodied client on a gurney for a trip to the emergency room. As they were wheeling him out, he regained consciousness and said, "See, Raoul, the living God was right."

Avoiding Craziness

A friend recounted an incident that occurred when he started army basic training. A soldier in his platoon had conversations with a make-believe friend similar to Elwood P. Dowd's amiable chats with the giant invisible rabbit, Harvey. After the first week, the Army booted out the soldier on a Section Eight, a medical discharge. The dismissed recruit did not receive a dishonorable discharge, which would have represented a black mark on any future job application. Medical discharges, although not that common, were granted for asthma, allergies, or even for one man I knew whose feet swelled inside army boots.

Years later, my friend ran into another guy who had been in the same basic training platoon and who also served in the army reserve. They commiserated about the long five-and-a-half-year reserve commitment, with its two weeks of summer camp each year and the boring, monthly weekend meetings. They reminisced about basic training and enjoyed a good laugh remembering the odd soldier, also a reservist, who chatted with his invisible pal.

But then my friend had an unpleasant thought: What if the loony recruit had faked the craziness knowing that a Section Eight awaited him, along with the elimination of any long-term reserve time? Was he crazy or was he sane?

The point of the story is that in the law, in life, and in the military, no one wants to deal with a person acting crazy.

SUMMING UP

Not everyone has the natural ability to negotiate; it takes learning and patience. Some people have an "ear" for languages, and I would also say that some have an "ear" for negotiation as well. Nevertheless, you can develop fluency and become successful at negotiations if you learn a few, easy rules and follow the same advice artists hear on how to get to Carnegie Hall—practice, practice, and more practice.

You might believe that negotiation is a fair and reasonable method to expedite the settlement of all aspects of social interaction. But there are two themes in which this is not the case: One is the area of bad negotiations, and the second comprises issues that fall into a nonnegotiable category.

Bad Negotiations

Bad or superfluous negotiations become accidents waiting to happen. They serve as reminders of the old proverb, "A bird in the hand is worth two in the bush." These instances tend to go beyond avarice or overachievement; they are bad decisions promulgated by delusion or idiocy, or both.

I represented a wealthy man in a divorce action who settled a wonderful lump-sum payment on his wife along with a large house and generous child support for their three children up to and beyond graduate school. The split-up was amicable and civilized, and both parties proceeded to get on with their lives.

Over the next five years, the man's successful business took a sharp upswing, taking him from being a comfortable millionaire up to being a multi-mega-buck millionaire. His wealth burgeoned, and being a considerate person, he decided to share his newfound riches with his ex-wife and children. Specifically, he offered to buy them a new house up to $2 million, to purchase her a new car up to $50,000, and also to grant his ex-spouse $150,000 cash a year until the youngest child left the nest. These generous gifts stemmed from the goodness of his heart and not from any previously contracted step-deal tied to increased income.

Did the ex-wife gush with gratitude at her serendipitous largesse? Did she make his favorite dinner and bake an apple pie? No, the former spouse laughed in her ex-husband's face and then hired an attorney to set aside the original agreement and to sue for an even larger share of his new wealth.

Back into court we went; and after trial, the judge ruled that the wife was not entitled to one additional penny over and above the original divorce settlement. The husband withdrew his offers of cash, car, and house because the wife had slapped his generosity in the face and forced him to return to court.

What could have prompted her action? Did the woman listen to the clack of mercenary Iagos urging her to return to court and demand a larger settlement? Had she become self-delusional without outside prompting?

Similarly, a wife received bad publicity and came off poorly in the press in a famous New York case concerning an existing prenuptial agreement. She consulted me and I told her how to fix matters with the media, and the strategy worked. She then asked if I could renegotiate a new settlement. I said she would have to deal with the reality of the prenuptial agreement she had already signed. She replied cavalierly, "Oh, that prenup is not worth the paper it is written on." I chose not to represent her since she was delusional, or perhaps in denial, about the law. She expended a lot of money and time with another lawyer, and even then, the court did not grant her any remedy different from the original prenuptial contract.

Nonnegotiable Matters

There are certain areas where not even the most expert negotiation can induce a decision. These are related to the most private of matters such as religion, nationality, and parenthood.

I have heard of exceptionally rare custody cases where one party (invariably, a rich father or wealthy and spiteful grandparents) will offer a mother an enormous sum to give up the child with the proviso of never seeing her offspring again. Most women will turn down the bag of gold and will not sell their baby at any price. Even if such a deal secretly offered some attraction, the prospect of public obloquy would tend to prevent it from happening. Motherhood and abandonment cannot be placed on the table for negotiation. But some horrible people will try.

A former divorce client, the elder of two daughters, and an attractive and successful magazine and book writer, grew up favored by both parents. Her younger sister harbored hateful sibling rivalry and expressed lifelong anger against both parents, but especially toward the mother.

When the widowed mother died in a Philadelphia nursing home, my client, who was lecturing at Toronto University, flew back for the funeral and cremation. She stayed for a few days and then had to return to her summer teaching assignment in Canada. The younger sister could keep or get rid of all of the mother's possessions.

While reviewing old documents and papers, the younger sister discovered that 20 years earlier the mother had given my client 15 family quilts, dating back 150 years, with instructions to donate them to the American Craft Museum in New York City and to take the charitable tax deduction as her own. The younger daughter fumed; even after the mother's death, she felt slighted and, worse, cheated out of her share of the quilts.

The sister wrote to my client, demanding that the two of them sue the museum for the return of the quilts (which in the intervening years had appreciated fourfold, perhaps even five-fold). Her reasoning was that she was entitled to half ownership of these valuable family heirlooms. My client refused to embark on any litigation.

What did the younger sister try to negotiate? She would only consent to return the mother's ashes if both sisters pursued legal action against the American Craft Museum. If there was no jointly filed suit, she would never surrender the urn for burial.

My client affirmed she would not be blackmailed into this futile and dim-witted action; their mother's ashes were non-negotiable.

I had a case representing a husband whose wife became a Jehovah's Witness and was raising their son in that faith. The child accompanied the mother on proselytizing visits to homes and communities and even stood in Grand Central Station, hand-ing out the sect's familiar *Watchtower* booklet.

We tried to negotiate a reasonable compromise in which the child would be free of some of the sect's more stringent rules (e.g., no celebration of Christmas). We hoped that giving the child some choice would reduce the mother's rigid control. But the wife did not consider religious freedom part of the settlement and refused to listen to any of our entreaties. It is an example of disputes that are almost never amenable to rational discussion or to settlement.

I had another case that was appealed to the highest court in the New York State. We originally represented a mother who did not believe in having her children vaccinated against smallpox or any other disease. She also believed that electricity gave off injurious rays and wanted to move to an isolated cabin without electricity in the Adirondack Mountains of New York.

We admonished the mother that unless she agreed to some resolution of her vaccination and electricity concerns, she would lose custody of the children. I gave her a heads-up warning by repeating the judge's remark. He said, "Tell this woman that at trial we are not going to turn off the lights in the courtroom." She was adamant about her rights and beliefs, and we had to advise her to find another attorney, which she did—and ended up losing custody.

The most famous nonnegotiable quote emanated with World War II Brigadier General Anthony McAuliffe, who responded to the German demand for surrender during the Battle of the Bulge with the well-remembered word, "Nuts!"

The Last Word

In the final analysis, good negotiation is the art of the possible. With proper negotiation, the possible becomes the probable, and with superb negotiation, the probable becomes the certainty of success.